Soil Sweat 'n' Tears

Advice For Reluctant Gardeners

by

Brian Carline

Illustrated by DAVID SUMMERVILLE

**Grosvenor House
Publishing Limited**

This book is published by
Grosvenor House Publishing Ltd
28-30 High Street, Guildford, Surrey, GU1 3HY.
www.grosvenorhousepublishing.co.uk

A CIP record for this book
is available from the British Library

ISBN 978-1-907652-25-7

Dedication

*To my wife, Christine,
the best weeder in the world.*

Happy gardening!

Best wishes

B. Clie

ACKNOWLEDGEMENTS

Richard Evans for his nanotechnology skills.

My friends at Essex Pelargonium Society.

My fellow allotment holders and gardeners for their inspiration.

Contents

INTRODUCTION

To some, the term gardening has an apocalyptic ring to it. This word is often associated with a sense of unwanted duty, feelings of apathy and procrastination. Others take the short-sighted view that gardening means digging and all of its related aches and pains. This kind of pessimism was offered to me when I recently visited a friend, whose passion and confidence in all matters connected with gardening was equivalent to that of a Flamenco dancer being asked to perform in a condemned building.

My friend's wife enquired of him, 'It's your sixtieth birthday next week. What do you want to do for it?'

'Oh, I don't know, Hilda,' he said impatiently. 'Take me somewhere we haven't been for long while.'

'How about the back garden, George?' came her sarcastic riposte.

Gardening needn't be a mystery or, indeed, viewed as an unenviable chore. The words 'little and often' constitute an empirical law that applies to all aspects of garden husbandry. Gardening is entitled to become a euphemism for agony and misery when this rule is not employed.

Television gardening programmes have come a long way since the days of the sagacious Percy Thrower and my utilitarian hero, Geoff Hamilton. Today we are saturated with advice from a multitude of horticultural geniuses whose landscape ideas range from minimalist to the **über-funky**. Though some of their creations are at odds with my personal taste, we all share a common recommendation that you should treat your garden as an extra room of your house. The majority of us would not allow our lounge or dining room to accumulate rubbish or look untidy. Regular short tasks of sweeping and tidying maintain pleasant and liveable surroundings. A garden should be no different. It too will benefit from routine short bursts of attention, such as mowing the lawn or trimming the hedge.

Quite understandably, gardening will feel like hard work when this part of the house is neglected for a long period. If there comes a time when the grass is waist-high and you can no longer see your garden shed, then even you will have to agree with your spouse that order should be restored.

You will certainly be privy to plenty of advice and opinion applying to all garden craft. An old gardener once told me that the soil was ready for sowing seeds when you could sit your bare bottom on the soil and you wouldn't feel uncomfortably cold and wet. I quickly dispensed with his irresonsible words after being reported to the police for repeatedly dropping my trousers on my allotment plot.

Most gardening folklore gems relate to weather:-
'Oak before Ash – We're in for a splash.'
'Ash before Oak – We're in for a soak.'

" A unique way to test your soil"

In simple terms this attempt at poetry refers to leaf budding and to the degree of ensuing rainfall. Since retiring and now having time to observe trees for long periods, I have discovered there is some meteorological truth in this maxim. There is also truth in the adage, 'Those who stare at trees for hours need to get a life.'

Another priceless prophecy imparted to me by a flat-nosed and somewhat deluded philosopher warned both myself and fellow allotmenters:

'If you drop your rake and it lands prongs up, it'll rain next day!'

As a postscript to his prediction, I saw him drop his rake prongs up on many occasions and not once was there a downpour... merely the sound of a sudden and painful thud as the handle smashed against his face when he stepped on the thing.

Gardening is a pleasure when the end result you have achieved for minimum labour is both pleasing to the eye and easy on your wallet. A neat, tidy and colourful garden is the ideal environment to help you relax and unwind. I was encouraged when I read words from a gentleman whom I believed to have become a recent gardening convert. Alas, a final sentence reflected his uncanny antipathy for the subject. He wrote:

'There's no finer place to be than your garden on a summer's day and to behold such a multitude of colours. To lie back and enjoy the sun as its rays gently kiss your face. To listen to the birds singing and, most important of all, to have the comforting knowledge that the lawnmower's broken.'

You may consider gardening an alien subject because you do not understand it. Anything green or which produces flowers continues to be an enigma. The purpose of this book is to take the mystique out of garden theory and practice. It provides you with simple tips and elementary advice on how to create and maintain a manageable garden.

Much emphasis is currently placed on healthy eating. Being able to grow some pesticide-free fruit and vegetables is certainly a bonus. Once more, such an undertaking does not demand a qualification in molecular biology. Comprehensive and practical tips provided in this book will help improve your cachet with the family as you serve up a salad from your tiny vegetable patch. Uncomplicated information, dispensed by the chapter on growing your own, will not only contribute to a healthy diet but also reduce the family food bill.

Gardening is also a means of taking exercise. Regular exercise is but one way of securing the good health we crave, thereby achieving the slowest possible rate at which we approach our demise. Exercise physiologists say that gardening improves cardiovascular fitness and is good for muscles and joints. However, a gardening sceptic once described garden craft as a chore conducted by people who have a cast iron back with a hinge in it. He also claimed the medical term 'growing pains' should be reserved solely for those who garden.

It is true that on occasions we have to bend or kneel to minister to our plants. Another golden rule is 'not to overdo it'. I know an 80-year old Yorkshireman who practises the principle of the conservation of energy relating to gardening protocol.

'Whenever I have to bend down, lad,' he says, 'I always look for summat else to do whilst I'm down there.'

Gardening can be included as part of your general fitness programme, although with advancing years you will notice that nature does slow you down. In my case, tasks that would have taken me twenty minutes, twenty years ago, now take me twenty minutes longer. My wife reckons I need potting on.

You may feel you are someone with an atrocious horticultural reputation. Take no notice if neighbours refer to you as the only gardener who can make a perennial become an annual with the swipe of a spade. Do not let this dishearten you. The easy guidance in the following chapters will give you both confidence and optimism. You will then understand what you are doing and be proudly able to create your own Garden of Eden... but get someone in to deal with the serpent.

Reluctant gardeners and other interested applicants, please read on.

1

GARDEN TOOLS

In these days of gadgets and gizmos, many apprentice gardeners see such new and quirky instruments as a solution to their horticultural needs. I witnessed a gardening virgin attempt to use a remote-controlled lawnmower the size of two shoeboxes to cut his large rear lawn. He sat back in his sun lounger and proceeded to operate this hideous contraption like a man possessed. The rather anaemic results produced by such an inappropriate and inadequate machine forced the said gentleman to abandon it after two hours and sadly sing the ditty, 'I fought the lawn and the lawn won.' In short, for years the majority of us have managed our garden chores with a small range of helpful, yet inexpensive, tools.

If you are new to the gardening scene, there is no point in spending huge sums of money on garden implements. The basics for any provincial gardener are spade, digging fork, Dutch hoe, rake, garden line, dibber, knife, wheelbarrow, watering can, trowel and a pair of secateurs. Visit any car boot sale and you will pick up the majority of these instruments very cheaply. Take them home and keep them secure. This will avoid someone else

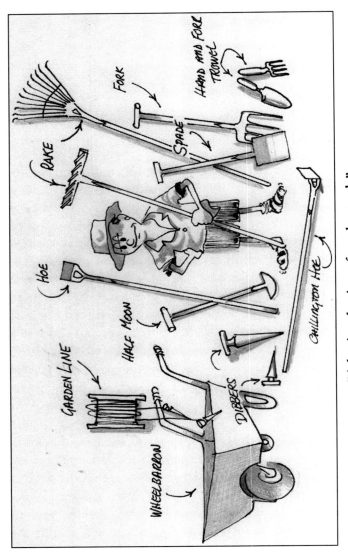

"A basic selection of garden tools"

2

repurchasing them at a boot sale a couple of weeks later, from the burglar who recently liberated them from your shed.

The above tools are the ideal practical starter kit. They will help you do the jobs you need to undertake in your garden. It's often wise to check the 'for sale' section of your local newspaper for garden tools. You can frequently pick up real bargains, though if you haven't heard of the tool and the advert reads 'hardly used', then the object in question is probably useless. Someone once gave me a gadget billed as 'the garden claw', guaranteed to break open the toughest of ground. The device sits in the back of my shed, as it has done for the last fifteen years. My wife witnessed my initial unsuccessful use of this instrument and shouted 'Oh, fork it, Brian! Fork it!' I never knew her capable of such appalling language. Nevertheless, I decided to take her advice and found the humble garden fork easier to use and give better results.

After you have used any garden tool, I would always advise cleaning it. This means you won't have this job to do before you next use it, and such good practice will allow your garden implements to have an extended life. In the long term this simple routine will save you money. Use an old kitchen knife or paper scraper to remove stubborn soil and mud.

I have witnessed lazy gardeners leave wooden-handled forks or spades outside over the winter months. Such poor husbandry can lead to accidents next time they are used. A rotten shaft of a garden fork can cause you to fall over as it cracks under your weight. It may give your children or neighbour a laugh, but I am sure you will not share the humour as you tumble into the rose bushes.

The digging fork is, perhaps, the tool you will use most frequently. It can double as a spade. It enables you to turn over the ground and break it up into small clods. If you want to encourage members of your family to assist in garden maintenance, you can always purchase smaller, border forks. They look less daunting and less energy consuming. Spades are essential though, if you are digging ground littered with large stones. If you use a fork on such ground, there is danger of you bending its prongs.

The simple wheelbarrow according to the laws of physics is, in fact, a lever. It allows you to undertake work more easily. Wheelbarrows come in different shapes and sizes and it is vital you have one to match the jobs you intend to do. By far the best is a builder's barrow. Admittedly, it does not look stylish and will give you little prestige as you tend your topiary in the Home Counties, but it is durable and can cope with anything from manure to paving slabs. The beauty of such a tool is that it has a broad, inflatable tyre and makes pushing it much easier. Beware of rose and fruit bush thorns if you are to avoid puncture repairs. Avoid barrows with a narrow wheel and solid tyre. These contraptions have little strength and will cut a furrow in your lawn each time you use it under load. Frequent use in wet weather makes your lawn resemble a ploughed field. Flimsy barrows made of fabric or plastic rarely last the course.

A rake is an essential tool, particularly if you are starting your garden from scratch. It allows you to get a fine tilth

"Stepping on a rake can be a painful experience"

and separates out clods of earth that can then be further broken down. It also filters out stones. Remember, your rake can be used as a spreader, particularly if you use both edges. However, when you finish using it, stand it upright and not at an angle. Do not leave it on the ground with its teeth facing you. There are many toothless gardeners with lips like Atlantic monkfish, all having ignored this safety tip. Stepping on a rake is a most unpleasant error to make.

The Dutch hoe, when in the correct hands, can be a real bonus tool for removing weeds in flower or vegetable beds. Not only does it scythe through these unwanted plants, but it also brings air into the soil and lessens soil compaction. However, if you are uncoordinated or find it difficult to put rope through the eye of a harpoon, then I would refrain from using such a utensil. This will avoid lacerating your lettuce or lopping your lobelia as you attempt to create a weed-free garden. Father Christmas is a genuine advocate for the use of this tool. 'Hoe, hoe, hoe, everybody!' is his seasonal guidance.

I have had my galvanized watering can for the last twenty years. God willing, it will continue to serve me for a similar time span. It is a little battered, looking as though it was relieved at Mafeking, but it does its job. The only problem with a watering can is the fact that you can easily lose its rose. I now make a point of always replacing this artefact on the spout of the can immediately after use. Such reflex practice has come about after years of trying to remember where I had left it.

A rose makes a watering can. Without a decent rose, you may just as well throw a bucket of water over your plants.

"Use a fine rose for watering seedlings"

A fine rose is absolutely necessary for watering seeds or seedlings. Cheap cans usually possess a rose with a few rings of wide bore holes, capable of emitting jets of water similar to a hosepipe. These objects may be suitable for irrigating established shrubs or bedding plants, but not for finer and more delicate work. Haws make a range of cans regarded by many as the Rolls Royce of the watering world. They possess a brass rose, with tiny holes giving you a fine spray. They will last you ages. Try persuading the kids to club together to buy you one for your birthday. However, there is one common problem with all roses. They will block with leaf debris if you leave them outside. The rotting sediment then lodges in the holes of the rose and will give an uneven and often anaemic spray next time you use them. Keep your can in the shed over the winter period to avoid this problem and give it a good rinse out before you put it to use.

A garden knife is yet another important tool for any gardener. I always carry a penknife in my pocket for opening fertilizer bags, cutting twine or small branches. Now that the children are grown up, I also leave an old bread knife in the ground for cutting lettuce and cabbages. Again, to avoid misplacing it, always leave it in the same place. A good knife can also help you dead-head flowers. If you really catch the propagation bug, a sharp knife can be used to take cuttings. If you are less ambitious, then stick to using it for sharpening your garden pencil.

Some fifty years ago, while at secondary school, I recall making an object called a dibber during woodwork classes. Having been raised in the United Kingdom's most industrialized city where the sole patch of greenery was Old Trafford, neither I, nor any of my classmates, knew of a use for this dibber. Our woodwork teacher exhibited all of the personal attributes of Josef Mengele, so nobody had the courage to ask. I thought the word dibber was something to do with the Boy Scout movement and used for erecting tents.

The simple T-shaped dibber is an asset in the vegetable garden for making holes to plant your greens, lettuce and leeks. It can also be useful for planting small bulbs in the flower border. Don't buy one. A broken shaft of a fork or spade can easily be whittled to produce a useful dibber. You can achieve deep holes when you push on its handle. I know someone who even uses a cricket stump and a hammer to bed in his winter leeks and brassicas.

Tidy gardeners understand the need for a garden line. If you are sowing seeds, planting flowers or vegetables, you will find this guideline invaluable. We have come a long way from the feudal mechanism of randomly broadcasting seeds, and thanks to the imagination and wisdom of Jethro Tull, farmers now plant and sow in straight lines. Young plants are far easier to tend in neat lines. Similarly, this simple garden line will be of use for giving you straight edges on your lawn and any landscaping work. Once more, there's no point in purchasing such an essential. Two pieces of wood connected by some string will suffice. A good practical tip is to always wind the string onto one of the stakes after use. This will prevent knots and twists occurring in it, gradually reducing its length. Keep it out of the rain and your line won't rot. A garden line should last a few seasons before you need to replace the string.

Secateurs can vary in quality and you can be tempted to pay a lot of money for a pair. I prefer to use the parrot-bill type. They should only be used for cutting through small branches and there is often a danger of overstretching your secateurs, particularly the ratchet type. You will damage these instruments if you try to hack through a thick branch that should have been tackled with a lopper or pruning saw. If you try and twist the secateurs when you are cutting, then you are using them incorrectly. You should aim for clean cuts and not to cut and rip branches. Pruning jobs require the use of secateurs and nowadays even left-handed models are available. Again, a good pair of secateurs should last years if you look after them. Oil and sharpen them when necessary.

In time you will add to your garden tool collection. Second-hand tools can be purchased cheaply. Your repertoire may include a mattock, bow saw, pruning saw, onion hoe and edging shears. A tool that is commonly regarded as the most used implement throughout the world is the garden cultivator. It can be seen in different guises, but the most widely used form is the Chillington hoe. This will easily break up ground, particularly clay soils. There is also a fork version of this hoe, and again this can be a bonus when breaking up soil before planting.

An onion hoe is an efficient implement when in the right hands. It has a small reflex blade that can scythe through

"Don't overstretch your secateurs"

weeds in between the plants you wish to thrive. They were originally made to weed in between onion bulbs. The beauty of this tool is that it not only cuts through the aerial parts of the weed, but can also gouge its roots as well as turning over the soil, adding air.

Power tools are now big business. There seems to be a power tool for every gardening job. Whether they are petrol or electrically-driven, treat them with respect and always read the safety advice. Electric power tools demand the use of an RCD. Never attempt to use one without this life-saving device.

A power tool that should never be used by the amateur gardener is a chainsaw. I am appalled by the number of untrained and ingenuous local residents whom I hear using these lethal weapons on Sunday mornings. There are never any minor injuries caused by chainsaws. Leave such tree work to the professional tree surgeon. Ignore these words and you may need to employ the skills of a transplant surgeon.

Power hedgecutters can be a pleasure to use. They really do reduce the time taken to clip a privet hedge, and give excellent results. However, remember the safety guidelines and wear eye protection, helmet and gloves. To some people these recommendations may sound unnecessary. However, professional gardeners use them and so should you. Cheap two-stroke petrol hedgetrimmers can easily cope with most garden hedges, although some sound as if Evel Knievel is riding up and down your back lawn. I gave up with an electric hedgetrimmer because of my predisposition for

"Leave chain saws to the professionals"

severing its cable. I cut more cords than a maternity unit midwife. If you must pare your hawthorn and privet hedge with an electric trimmer, then develop a cutting technique that enables you to know the whereabouts of the cable.

If there is something about managing a large garden that really annoys me, it is hosepipes. I have yet to discover one that is absolutely kink-resistant. Cheap hosepipes go rigid in cold weather and are reluctant to change shape. They proceed to knock over tubs and pots when you drag them from place to place. Supple pipes twist and crimp, reducing the water flow. I once counted five kinks in a run of a 50-foot hose. Roll up your hose in the autumn when you have finished with it. Choose a mild day and it will coil better. Hosepipe adapters that allow you to vary the spray are most welcome additions for your irrigation duties.

I am frequently amused by the fact that people will still look down a hosepipe to see why water does not appear to be emerging from the end of it. I can think of a more hygienic way to wash your face.

You can now purchase environmentally-friendly wheelie bins suitable for disposing of your garden debris. They are decorated with a montage of leaves and twigs and are designed to blend in with your garden and reduce the 'eyesore' effect of these depositories. A chap in our village bought one of these bins and their camouflage proved so effective it took him weeks to discover where he had left it.

Other gadgetry you may decide to acquire over the years may be garden vacs for blowing or collecting garden leaves. If you do prefer a lazy life, then these machines are for you. Similarly, the butane weeder allows you to burn weeds as you walk through your garden without having to bend down. Again, be careful with this accoutrement and do not use them while wearing sandals or in bare feet. This will avoid barbecuing your toes and alerting your neighbours that you know some pretty awful swear words. These incendiary tools will only destroy the visible part of the weed and possibly leave its root intact. This is particularly true for aggressive, perennial weeds.

I frequently see garden shredders for sale in my local newspaper. This would tend to suggest that people buy them expecting they will compost everything from leaves to branches. Indeed, they will cope with garden leaves and will give you a shredded end product that will rapidly compost. However, most domestic shredders will not cope with branches and will jam or soon blunt their cutting surfaces. I really do not see the need for them, leaves compost well on their own. If you must spend your money on such a contraption, don't expect too much from them and remember safety issues. Do not shred wearing a scarf or tie for obvious reasons.

Another popular instrument owned by nearly everyone these days is the power washer. They are effective for cleaning algae and grime-covered patios. They can even be used for cleaning and rejuvenating garden furniture. I would add words of caution, however, when attempting to restore transparency to your greenhouse or cold frames. Old horticultural-grade glass becomes

"Never use a shredder when wearing a scarf"

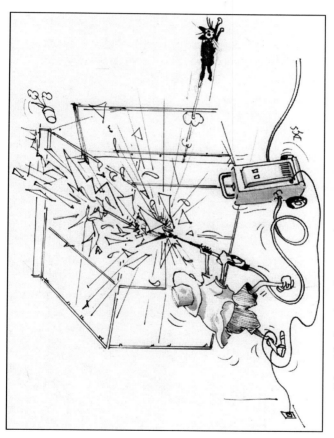

"Avoid cleaning the greenhouse with a power washer"

brittle with time and your irrigation technique may cost you many replacement panes of glass. Stick to drives and garden paths.

Should you be tempted to borrow tools, then always keep in mind that other people's tools work best in other people's gardens. Should you damage or destroy them it can be quite embarrassing when you return the broken instrument. Statements like: 'Oh, that's alright, it was an old pair anyway!' will really be a disguised riposte for: 'Can't that flamin' idiot of a bloke do anything right?'

Whatever you do concerning your garden tools, never be tempted to throw in the trowel. Happy gardening!

The Ten Commandments for Garden Tools

1. Start your garden tool collection by purchasing decent second-hand tools.
2. Make sure you have in your collection a garden spade, fork, Dutch hoe, rake, garden line, knife, wheelbarrow, watering can, hosepipe, trowel and a pair of secateurs. Slowly add to your repertoire of tools by including a mattock, pruning saw, cultivator and an edging tool.
3. Always clean your tools after use and lock them away in a secure place.
4. A robust builder's barrow can be used for many jobs, from carrying bags of compost to knocking up mixes of sand and cement for landscaping jobs.
5. Buy a watering can with a fine rose for watering seeds and young seedlings.

6. Make some of your own tools such as a dibber and garden line. Use an old kitchen knife for cutting vegetables, twine and plastic fertilizer bags.

7. Don't try to cut through branches that are too big for your secateurs. It's just as much hard work for them as it is for you and you will injure both parties in the process.

8. If you can't get on with two-stroke petrol engines, then it's electric power tools for you. In both instances, follow the safety guidelines.

9. Leave the use of chainsaws to the professionals.

10. Should a neighbour ask if they could use your lawnmower, then encourage them to do so but add the caveat that it must not be taken out of your garden. They won't ask again.

Remember, all gardeners should call a spade a spade until they trip over one.

2

LAWN CARE

Michael Pollan once advised that a lawn is nature under totalitarian rule.

You do not need the landscaping mind of Capability Brown to produce a decent lawn. The first question you must ask yourself is, 'Why do I need this verdant area?' If the answer is to play croquet or invite the gang from the local bowls club around for an important league match, then you will need to take out a bank loan or consider cashing in your premium bonds.

If, in common with the majority of us, you would like an area that looks green, tidy and somewhere for the kids to re-enact the World Cup, then your financial commitment will be less onerous. It is the sensible and practical option. I overheard a chauvinist estate agent advising an equally chauvinistic male client that he should never have a lawn bigger than his wife can manage. I thought my wife was going to whack him with her umbrella!

Should you inherit a lawn that looks so tired even the local cat population refuse to use it as a toilet, this does not bode well. You will have plenty to do. However, once this rejuvenation and invigoration process has been achieved, to maintain its good looks and appearance will not put you in hospital or drive you to drink.

A neglected and overgrown lawn may simply need a renovation programme. Nevertheless, if you realize this patch has received no attention for years - having discovered a woolly mammoth in some of the vegetation - then it's probably wise to start from scratch.

Spring is the best time for any renovation programme and the first thing you must do is to cut the grass and weeds down to a couple of inches above ground level. If the area you are attempting to change has grass as tall as the Serengeti, then you must use shears or, for an easier life, a strimmer. However, I would add words of caution here. Always use a strimmer that's right for the amount of strimming you have to do. An edging, electric version is no use for tackling an out-of-control area the size of a tennis court. The task would take you years and the machine would burn out after an hour. Similarly, be careful when using the heavy-duty petrol types. The cutting nylon is thick and has impressive slicing abilities. I recall one overzealous lawn maker, during a lapse in concentration, removing the tips from his trainers followed by cracking several panes of his glass cold frame. Never strim in sandals, flip flops or bare feet. Similarly, no-one yearns for the facial appeal of a Cyclops, so always wear eye protection. Strimmers can flick up stones and twigs at supersonic speeds.

Should someone suggest using a scythe, ignore their irresponsible words. Scything is a specialized operational skill and not for the amateur. If you are happy with your current height, or that of someone close by, then leave this implement for the sole use of the Grim Reaper.

Your next job is to clear these clippings. It's easy to use a rake and broom for this chore. The rake will draw the cut grass into manageable mounds, and a besom or birch broom allows you to remove the rest of the fine debris. You possibly last used one of these at Hallowe'en or perhaps your mother-in-law left it behind after her last flying visit.

In most cases your lawn will look better for simply doing this. Should you find specific problems such as craters and bumps, you will have to remedy these eyesores before you can continue. Do not try to flatten any bumps with a sledgehammer or by using a two hundredweight garden roller. It may look good superficially, but you will have compacted the soil. The terrain will now be void of air and water. Earthworms will now suffer concussion or irreparable brain damage. The grass, for which you ultimately yearn, will not grow in an area that has been treated like an anvil. Sadly, you will have to dig away such mountainous sections and replace the new flat top surface with some decent topsoil. Similarly, any dips in your lawn will need attention. Fill the hollow with topsoil and firm down just enough to receive a new turf or provide a key for new grass seed. Work done on these two problems now will make life easier for you in the future. For example, you won't scalp the lawn when trying to mow over a bump, and your mowing efforts

"Never remove bumps in your lawn with a power hammer"

won't come to a full stop as you disappear into a crater near the garden shed.

If your lawn is used by ants and moles, they will leave you with tell-tale signs. These two lawn pests can deposit mounds of earth as they burrow away. I remember visiting a colleague's garden that looked at first glance like the battlefields of Verdun. Such devastation was caused by a trio of small mammals who answered to the name of Talpa europaea (the common garden mole) and not to names such as 'bastards' and 'little bleeders'. These creatures have to go, otherwise you will be flogging the proverbial dead horse. Numerous prescriptions for their removal have been formulated over the years, from garlic pellets and mothballs to toxic gas and sonic shock. Mole traps, when set in the correct way, seem to be the remedy. The natural predators of these industrious earthmovers are badgers and ferrets. One surefire way of assisting the relocation of these moles is to drop some badger or ferret poo into one of their tunnels. Unfortunately, you may have a problem acquiring such faeces. Try Ebay, you seem to be able to buy anything on there these days. Should all of these fail, you may be tempted to use a shotgun. Life should never get you down this much. Think of the wife and kids!

It is now time to cut your lawn for the first time. The cardinal sin is to set your mower blades too low. I can understand why people do this. Their logic being that the shorter it is cut, the longer it will take the grass to grow back. Unfortunately such wisdom comes back to haunt you. Scalping a lawn does a number of things. It prevents the grass leaves from making sufficient food for the plant

"Leave troublesome moles to the mole catcher"

to grow properly and weakens the root system. It also causes the ground to dry out rapidly, and both of these issues cause yellow patches with poor grass growth. I once witnessed a neighbour whose passion for gardening was equivalent to having a molar tooth pulled without an anaesthetic. He dropped his blades so low that when his cylinder mower attempted to manicure his 20 foot by 30 foot sea of green, he proceeded to disappear into the earth's crust and shower his neighbours with thatch and soil particles. Similarly with rotary mowers. If you find the science of crop circles fascinating, try setting your cutting blade to rock bottom and then stand back and observe these phenomena.

It is advisable to empty the grass box or hopper each time you have finished cutting the lawn. Some reluctant gardeners can't be bothered and leave the clippings inside, only to discover a putrid mass swarming with insect ephemera the next time their lawn is due for a trim. Such malpractice does little for your enthusiasm or your nostrils.

I remain pessimistic about mowers with no receptacle for collecting the grass you cut. Your lawn will always look untidy if you use such a device. Their unique selling point may be that you do not have to empty the grass box, but you soon find yourself wading through swathes of debris on the surface of the lawn. Their propaganda reassures you this technique provides a potentially nutritious mulch for the lawn. These mini-haystacks are both unhelpful for lawn growth and also an eyesore. You will be most unpopular in your home when your spouse points out you have trodden half of Denby Dale into the living room.

"Beware of setting your mower blades too low"

If you have a fair sized lawn to cut, ensure you have the correct mower for the job. Cheap electric mowers may cope with small or modest sized lawns. These machines can vibrate themselves into an early grave, as parts fall off or break. Some models shake so much you feel you are suffering from the delirium tremens. Even after completing your mowing task, your constant shaking makes it impossible to find your mouth with a cup of tea. I once had a neighbour who possessed a similar contraption that would dislodge his false teeth each time he started the thing.

Also don't blame the grass if it lies down for the mower and then immediately pops up again as soon as it has passed. It pays to invest in a good quality lawnmower if you really want your lawn to look tidy.

Lawnmowers can also be used in the autumn for collecting fallen leaves. However, check the lawn first before you mow it. There is nothing worse than finding you have mowed through a decent hosepipe or blunted the blades on a brick that has mysteriously appeared from nowhere. Caution too when using electric mowers. Avoid electrocuting yourself by cutting through the cable. Remember the RCD device is for your safety. Similarly, remember some simple physics you learnt at school – ELECTRICITY and WATER DO NOT MIX. So, don't attempt to cut your grass when it's raining or let the electric mower fall into the pond.

Petrol lawnmowers benefit from regular servicing. It prolongs their active life. When enquiring about the cost of a service, be able to quote its make and model. If asked, 'What kind of mower do you have?' and your answer is, 'A red one,' this riposte will fail to provide the necessary information.

If you wish to stripe your lawn, remember your mower must have a roller. It is this structure that produces the stripes when you go up and down your lawn. Cutting your lawn in the same direction will yield zero stripes. It's often fun to stripe diagonally or criss-cross. I heard of one chap troubled with a prying neighbour. He became quite skilled at striping his lawn. He cleverly striped the words NOSEY GIT on the grass of his rear garden which was readily visible from the inquisitive neighbour's bedroom.

Some of us are accident-prone. My wife bought me a hard hat to use when I give the lawn a cut. I am forever failing to duck and avoid branches on the fruit trees in my garden. So frequent were my collisions that, with so many plasters on my scalp, my kids said I looked deranged. Sporting my new headgear I now appear less like the victim of a road accident and more like one of the Village People.

Once you are satisfied with your mowing efforts, remember that during the summer - particularly when rain is followed by sunny spells - your lawn will grow fast and furious. You may be expected to cut it twice a week. At no time should mowing become an exhausting exercise. If this is the case, you are either leaving it too long between cuts or you are suffering from asthma or angina.

As a postscript to the topic of lawn cutting, a neighbour once asked my wife the question, 'Any chance of borrowing your lawnmower this Saturday?'

"Some have fun when striping their lawn"

'No problem,' she replied. 'He gets up at seven o'clock!'

Nowadays, there are plenty of products available that guarantee the greening up of your lawn. They are often called the lawn tonics because they contain plenty of nitrogen, the element commonly regarded as the leaf maker. To use these correctly, stick to the prescribed dilution otherwise they will seriously scorch the lawn. If you use granular lawn feeds, try to use them at a time when rain is expected; this will allow the chemicals to pass into solution and wash into the soil. If this irrigation is not achieved then again your grass will scorch. Accessories such as lawn spreaders are supposed to give you the correct application dose. This is particularly important when using lawn weed and feed preparations. These combinations are supposed to remove troublesome rosette weeds, such as dandelion or plantain, while at the same time provide your hungry grass roots with their necessary sustenance.

Lawn tonics can be extremely therapeutic. They are the Viagra of the plant world. However, I would not advise you to get the two bottles mixed up. In the garden, you could produce a lawn with grass leaves too stiff to mow and in the bedroom your naughty bits may turn green when you get excited.

If your gardening phobia shows a reluctance towards mowing the lawn, apply a generous dose of whisky to this area and the grass will come up half-cut!

You can attack any lawn problems in the autumn. Slow-acting fertilizers, fungicides and worm killers can all be applied at this time. Worms in any lawn can be an asset. They drag nutrients into the soil and make your soil more fertile and aerated. However, should you wake up each morning to a lawn resembling Blackpool beach at low tide, this is a sign they are taking over. You will then have to employ some anti-worming agent. A solution of washing-up liquid will do. They will quickly rise to the surface and thank you for giving them hands that do dishes! You can now relocate them to flower borders or the vegetable plot, or throw them onto your neighbour's lawn. There are only so many worm casts a person can tolerate.

I recently received a magazine providing suggestions for presents, aimed at those people who seem to have everything. On one of the pages I discovered 'Lawn Aerating Sandals'. Such sartorial accoutrements allow you to take the evening air and simultaneously spike and aerate your lawn. The plastic strap-on soles possess large shafts of metal designed to penetrate even the most stubborn lawns with such gusto that you produce a lawn which now has better drainage and a high proportion of earthworm kebabs. I dread to think what would happen to the Axminster in your living room if you were called inside to answer the telephone. Watch out too for hosepipes and underground power cables while sporting these prostheses.

If ever your relatives should unexpectedly threaten to pop round in the afternoon, you may find your lawn could do with a quick haircut. However, if you look at the timescale and decide there is not enough time for this procedure, one quick fix guaranteed to make

"Tread carefully when aerating your lawn"

the lawn look tidier, is to clip the edges. Use long-handled edging shears or an edging strimmer. Crisp, sharp edges to the lawn give it a neat and manicured appearance.

The use of a half-moon edging iron should be employed with care and an understanding that you are cutting soil with grass attached. Repeated use of this impressive tool could mean you reduce the area of your lawn considerably. I heard of one gardening enthusiast with a penchant for the half-moon, who slowly moved from a front lawn the size of a tennis court, to a neatly-edged green that would fill a Bonsai pot.

Establishing a decent, hardwearing lawn is not difficult. How to avoid making lawn care a backbreaking chore is to give the lawn attention little and often. Most people can find ten minutes at the weekend to keep on top of things; even those despairing citizens who have contemplated Astroturf or concrete as a solution to lawn management.

The Ten Commandments of Lawn Care

1. Choose the kind of lawn that fits its purpose. Luxury grade grasses do not wear well. Utility grade grasses have both practical and aesthetic qualities. If you are starting from scratch, it's probably better to turf the area rather than to seed it.
2. If the lawn you inherit is salvageable, start your rejuvenation programme by giving it a good haircut until you can inspect the area more closely.

Use tools that will work for you and make your job easier, such as strimmers. Shears can be hard work.

3. Buy yourself a leaf rake or besom to help clear the debris. These accessories will also come in handy during the autumn for raking dead leaves from your lawn.

4. Try to make the surface of your lawn as even as possible by making good any bumps and hollows. Work done now to remedy these problems will make your mowing simpler in the future and give you a uniform finish.

5. Treat yourself to a decent mower. Purchase one that is reliable and will not fall apart after a couple of years. Decide if you want petrol or electric, but remember the machine must match the job it has to do.

6. Don't cut your grass too short or allow your grass to grow too long. Both of these instances will generate problems.

7. If your lawn drains poorly, spike it with a garden fork. This will allow air into the soil as well as providing a means of draining excess water.

8. Use a feed and weed application. A spring and autumn attention should keep your lawn supplied with the nutrients it needs. It will also keep the pernicious weeds at bay. However, always keep to the prescribed dosage recommended by the manufacturers. Water in granular feeds if it doesn't rain.

9. Cut the edges of your lawn with edging shears or a small lightweight strimmer. It keeps the lawn looking neat and tidy. If you are tired after mowing, leave the edges until the following day.

10. Remember safety issues, particularly with any tools you use. Garden electrical appliances MUST be used with an RCD.

Once you have achieved a tidy and green lawn area, your gardening vocabulary will also improve. You will use the word 'sod' advisedly, as a piece of turf, and not as a profanity. Happy lawn care!

3

EASY-MAINTENANCE GARDENING

If the mere mention of the word gardening continues to precipitate feelings of terror and revulsion, perhaps a high-rise apartment or a life sailing the high seas is right for you. Indeed, should you show so much antipathy towards gardening and all things related, then living in a property with a large garden is as sensible as taking up goalkeeping if you suffer from rickets. Large gardens should really be reserved for people who have the time, money and inclination to look after them.

For the majority of us who have mortgages to pay and families to look after, there will only be a finite amount of time and pounds sterling to devote to our modest and unpretentious garden space. In these circumstances there will be a need for a garden that will provide an area for the children to play, as well as giving some seasonal colour and interest.

People look to 'low maintenance' gardening as the solution to their plight. My own take on this quick-fix term is that the more a garden becomes described as low maintenance, the less green and natural it becomes. As a landscape increases its low maintenance factor, there is

"Go easy on garden design ideas"

usually a proportionate rise in the use of concrete or similar building materials. Perhaps I feel more comfortable with the concept of easy maintenance gardening and one that allows a synergy to exist between nature, subsistence and functionality. Indeed, there may well be a need to use shingle or decking in your garden, but if you over-egg the pudding with these materials your back yard could resemble Chesil Beach or Dodge City respectively.

Do not be tempted to use tubs, troughs and baskets as a solution to lessen your commitment to gardening. These containers are positively high maintenance because of their constant demand for water and feed during warm weather. If you must include such features, then use compost with a wetting agent combined. Once peat-based composts dry out they are a real problem to rehydrate. Terracotta pots are porous and water will evaporate quickly from this surface on a hot, dry day. Line these pots with polythene or the plastic from compost sacks. This will help retain moisture within the soil. Ignore these two pieces of advice and you will embody Gunga Din as you endlessly travel back and forth with water. As one phlegmatic soul once said, 'Gardens need a lot of water and most of that is sweat.'

There are now irrigation mechanisms available that attach to your garden tap and drip feed water into containers and baskets. They are particularly useful if you go on holiday. Sometimes the tiny drip nozzle blocks with debris, so test this before you go. An alternative interpretation of drip feeding is to burden the drips who live next door and see if they will water your containers for two weeks while you enjoy yourself.

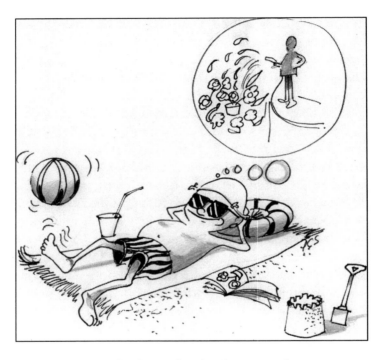

**"Drip feeding – let the drip next door
water your plants"**

People with busy lives, or those who live in parts of the country receiving a low rainfall, will often incorporate drought-resistant plants into their borders. Don't think that your garden will resemble the Death Valley if you do this. Nowadays there is a wide range of these drought tolerant plants available in garden centres. They often have grey, blue or silver leaves. Some have green, fleshy leaves with leathery or waxy coverings. Many exude fragrant oils. Some of their bright and colourful flowers can be seen opening up during the day, closing down by night. Lavenders, Cordylines, Blue fescue and Cistus (Rock Rose) are fine examples of plants for dry and sunny sites.

Should this kind of planting not be to your liking, think about laying a porous pipe along your borders, attached to your garden tap. Timers are now available that will control the watering for you. This will enable you to use more water-demanding species in your planting.

In any easy maintenance garden, I would recommend the use of alpines. Whether it's an alpine trough or a small rockery, these little beauties will provide you with colour year after year. They simply require well-drained soil and will then take care of themselves. Some alpines spread and provide excellent ground cover. Alpines can give spots of colour between stepping-stones or in dry stone walls. When you buy these plants, look at the pictures on the label and try to visualize them in your garden. There will also be information about growth habit and size.

As an easy maintenance gardener, you will no doubt be of the opinion that although hard work never killed anyone there's always a first time. It is, therefore, your duty to avoid time consuming and potentially life-threatening activities such as digging and weeding. One of the most important inventions pleasing any low energy gardener is weed suppressant membrane. This tough black material acts as an impenetrable barrier for weeds and should be spread on the surface of a soil border. You then place the plants you wish to include in this area on its surface. Cut a hole through the membrane and insert your plants into the soil. In the case of alpines, cover the membrane with shingle or gravel. The material will exclude light and prevent weeds growing through. Even tough and aggressive characters, such as twitch grass and ground elder, find the plastic difficult to assault.

This membrane can be used in other types of borders, but again cover the membrane with some material that prevents weed seeds from germinating and then establishing themselves. Commonly used examples of mulches are ornamental bark, slate and chippings.

Hardy perennials are a must for the easy maintenance garden. Once they are in, they stay there year after year with minimum fuss and attention. They die back after flowering, but return again to once more enliven your borders the following year. However, if you have little talent with colour matching or knowing what will look right when planted with other perennials, it may be worth employing someone who does know their onions. There is nothing more frustrating than planting up a border and then having to restructure it the following year because it doesn't look right. Do not confuse the term perennial with evergreen. The latter, as their name suggests, are woody plants that retain their leaves in winter. There are many fine examples of evergreens whose flowers and leaf colour provide an attractive inclusion in your easy care border. Typical examples of shrubs that need little attention will include rhododendrons, azaleas, pieris, choisyas and pitosporums.

Conifers are worthwhile evergreen inclusions in our easy upkeep garden. It is best to use slow growing varieties, then there is no worry about keeping them in check. They vary in growth habit and colours. There are golds, blues and all shades of green. Once more, when they are in, they are there to stay. Some conifers are susceptible to wind damage and most to extremes of drought. Prostrate forms spread well and can give excellent ground cover. Gentlemen! Do not confuse the word 'prostrate' with 'prostate'. This common malapropism will amuse your GP and do little for your street cred.

The hardy perennials will survive the winter but they die back only to reappear in the spring. You will find gaps in the herbaceous border during these cold months, but early flowering bulbs planted at the same time as your perennials will fill these temporary spaces. Hardy bulbs of all descriptions are vital inclusions for 'easy' gardening. Once more, when they are in, they will reward you each year with a dependable wealth of colour. Daffodils, narcissi and snowdrops are available with different flower heads and heights. Corms are bulb-like structures that survive in similar ways and they too have a whole range of colour, shapes and sizes. The crocus and cyclamens grow from these corms. If you do choose to incorporate bulbs and corms, make sure they are planted at the right depth. In this way they will have no problem in establishing themselves.

Gardening-shy individuals are tempted to plant roses in their gardens with the intention of filling spaces. They flower and seem to survive in perpetuity. Indeed, this concept is true but roses can spawn hard work. The majority need pruning and they are susceptible to disease, whether it is fungal or insect pest attack. If your partner demands their inclusion, go for a modern variety that clearly states its growth habit and disease resistance. If your knowledge of roses is poor and you think that a hybrid tea is a mixture of PG tips and Typhoo, then it is best to avoid them.

Bamboos and ornamental grasses can be used as excellent feature plants and demand little attention. However, choose non-invasive types that simply form clumps. There are tall and aggressive examples determined to convert your backyard into a Malayan panorama. They have no place in small gardens.

Bedding plants need lifting after they have completed their colourful summer lives. Bedding plants are high maintenance if you have a large garden, simply because you have to plant them in the late spring and then remove them in the autumn when the first frosts arrive. However, if you love striking colours then find ten minutes to include some in your borders. Remember, they demand plenty of water.

Any plants you choose for your easy care garden will need a reasonable soil and one that is fertile. Always include

"Some bamboo can take over your garden"

some organic material such as manure, mushroom compost or, if you must, some peat-based compost. Some time spent doing this before you plant will reward you in the future. When you plant these specimens, always use some slow release fertilizer. Fish, blood and bone is an excellent example of a long acting organic fertilizer. All you need do in six months' time is to sprinkle some around the base of the plant and allow the rain to take the nutrients to the roots. However, there are some lime intolerant plants. Heathers, rhododendrons, azaleas and camellias are lime prejudiced and so care should be taken to build up an acid soil around them. Ericaceous composts are now available at garden centres that do just this. They will also welcome a feed with a liquid sequestered iron fertilizer a couple of times a year. Sachets of this compound are also available off the shelf at garden centres. Hopefully, this treatment should prevent leaf yellowing and promote flowering.

A small patch of lawn is not asking too much for any reluctant gardener. To reduce labour, think about placing a lawn edging around the grass border. These structures are not cheap but always maintain a sharp edge to contain the grass. Mowing is all you need do, the edges are meant to keep their manicured look. I would avoid Astroturf or other forms of artificial lawn. Many look unnatural and manufactured. In my view, there is no substitute for grass. However, if it floats your boat, then why not?

Whenever you set out to design your easy fix garden, try to avoid future hard work for yourself. Think about how your garden tools will cope with your design. A good example here is when you decide to go for stepping-stones in a lawn; always sink them to the level of the lawn and your mower will cope with the cut and not blunt the blade. If you lay them on top of the grass, you will have to lift them each time you mow. It will also be necessary for you to put them back in exactly the same position to avoid yellow patches. Sinking them also avoids you tripping over them in the dark and falling through your greenhouse. If you choose wooden steps, remember they will be slippery when wet so cover them with some fine mesh chicken wire.

It is wise to keep your easy care lawn simple in shape and free from clutter. Mowing may not be your first love, so make it easy to perform. Avoid planting trees in the middle of your green sward or putting a big bench that requires relocating each time you mow. For most average easy care lawns the mowing process should take you no longer than ten minutes.

Another labour-saving tip is to create a bare strip or border where your lawn may meet a garden wall. This will enable the cutting blades of your mower to access the grass without it crashing against the brick face.

Any structure you include as a design feature or focal point needs to be sited correctly. By ensuring there is enough room for you to fit behind it, this will allow for ease of maintenance. A shed or gazebo needs a wood preservative coat every few years and if you cannot access the back panels, its life span will be greatly reduced. Greenhouses too often need a replacement pane and so allow a metre gap between it and your hedge.

"The effects of a tight squeeze"

This will avoid the sensation of being keel hauled as you try to squeeze between the structure and your hawthorn hedge.

On the subject of upkeep of outbuildings, a man knocked at my door and asked me, 'Do you want your garden shed re-tarred?' I was quite offended by his question and replied, 'Yes, I do, and I object to being called a retard!' The cheek of some people!

A garden hardscape could include the use of materials such as bricks, slabs, concrete, cobbles, shingle chippings, wood and bark. The key to the successful use of such ingredients is to get the balance right between plants, features and hard ground cover. Gardens that include much hard landscaping would be minimalist and Japanese style. Patios are relaxing places designed for you to enjoy the pleasanter times of the year. They too can be constructed using slabs or paving. Whenever you go down the road of using any of the above materials, always remember that it is hard work. Mixing large quantities of sand and cement is not the same as crocheting a blanket. Hard landscaping is a skilled job and, apart from being both time and energy consuming, it involves knowledge and appreciation of such things as levels, footings and drainage. Unless you are a DIY enthusiast and acquainted with these principles, I would employ a professional. It may be an expensive way to do it but it should give you pain-free peace of mind.

If continuous bending alarms you, then why not - as part of your new construction - build your beds and borders nearer to you? These raised beds will help in

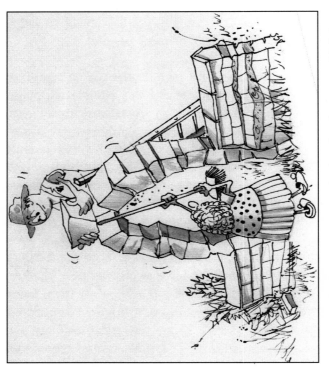

"Some DIY projects may be harder than you think"

further energy conservation and take the ache out of backache.

An unenthusiastic gardener who visits the back garden only when they have accidentally locked themselves out of the house, should not be persuaded to purchase a greenhouse or polytunnel. They are hard work and time consuming, even if it is to be a cold greenhouse used solely for growing tomatoes during the summer months. Greenhouses present problems with watering, pest management, temperature fluctuations and humidity. They require a commitment.

Some time ago I had the misfortune to visit a well-known stronghold for Chavs in Essex and overheard a loquacious member of this fraternity discussing how he would save the planet. His theory, punctuated with numerous expletives, was simple: 'If everyone's banging on about greenhouse gases being bad, then why do they still sell greenhouses?' QED.

The Ten Commandments of Easy-Maintenance Gardening

1. Do not flood your garden with tubs, pots, containers and baskets. These are high maintenance in terms of their watering and feeding.
2. Reduce weeding by covering your borders with weed suppressant membrane and then cover that with a thin mulch or dressing.
3. Build your borders so that they are easy to access and maintain. Include some drought tolerant plant types, as well as hardy perennials.

4. Include easy plants such as alpines for any tubs or ground cover. Build a small rockery and incorporate a range of these plants. Plant in groups of three if it is to be over a large area.

5. Include hardy bulbs alongside any perennials. These will flower and fill any gaps over the winter months.

6. Use evergreen shrubs for both foliage and flower colour. Avoid vigorous varieties that will need constant attention.

7. Conifers need little maintenance and provide all-year colour. Include some prostrate examples if you need plenty of ground cover.

8. Some areas of your garden will need watering more than others, particularly during periods of drought. Use a timer system that links to porous pipes or drip feeders.

9. Any lawn should be created so that it is easy to cut. Think of edges and where and how stepping-stones, benches and gazebos are placed.

10. Try to achieve the correct balance between the non-living landscape and the plants you choose. Realize your permanent easy care design may need some professional help from reputable landscapers. Some construction jobs demand expert help.

4

PRUNING

Pruning is a commonly used gardening term and gives to some a licence to mutilate and disfigure plant life. Invariably the reason for embarking on such a psychopathic exercise is due to apathy, fear or ignorance, the perpetrator having allowed their garden plants to grow unchecked over many seasons. Armed with bow saw, loppers, secateurs and even the fearsome chainsaw, our pruning terrorist sets out to reduce the dimensions of any plant that gets in his or her way, with alarming consequences. To avoid following such a naïve and damaging game plan, anyone who wishes to undertake successful pruning must keep in mind what pruning sets out to achieve.

Pruning is husbandry that should lead to good plant shape, healthy and disease-free growth and successful flowering and fruiting. If your pruning activities achieve none of these qualities and your garden resembles a recent nuclear attack, then it is time you read this chapter.

Pruning can be associated with elements of mystery and trepidation but you must always remember that plants are extremely resilient to whatever nature throws at

"Pruning need not be a mysterious art"

them. Within this context I include man's sometimes irresponsible attempts at pruning. In short, if you make a mess of your clipping and cutting exercises, your plants will usually recover with time. Unfortunately, there is no single recipe for pruning all plant types. Plants such as fruit trees are pruned in different ways to climbers. Even within a specific plant group there may be different ways of pruning them. However, there is a golden rule in pruning in that if you are unsure about how much to prune, too little is safer than too much.

Before any practical pruning is conducted, always have in mind how your victim should look after the pruning is complete. In other words, have a clear aim and sense of purpose about your pruning. Above all, if things seem to be going well, avoid the risk of becoming 'carried away' with your secateurs, particularly if you have just bought a new pair. Over-zealous pruners can often work against the principle of increasing the health, shape and vigour of a plant. If it is shape you want, it is worth stepping back occasionally to regulate and monitor your progress. However, I would not advise this technique if you are working up a ladder. Another essential recommendation is never to tackle pruning duties if you have just had the mother-of-all arguments with your partner. Many a clematis with a look of alopecia has resulted from a lunch-time domestic.

Remember, some established plants need very little pruning. Rhododendrons and similar plants such as choisya (Mexican orange blossom) need little attention. So, if it ain't broken then don't attempt to mend it. If you have planted a large growing variety that seems to constantly demand attention to keep it in proportion, the wisest thing is to replace it with a less vigorous form.

Privet and some other hedge plants may need frequent pruning in the summer months. At this point I must mention Cupressocyparis leylandii, known to many frustrated and troubled gardeners though as 'bloody leylandii'. This fast-growing conifer is frequently grown as a hedging plant. My personal opinion about this individual is that it should be treated like vermin or, if you are a schoolteacher, Ofsted. Such a plant will cause misery and anguish. It has no place in the domestic garden, so plant it at your peril. Certain climbers too may overpopulate a wall. Boston ivy with its broad leaves and adventitious roots (roots borne on a stem) can rapidly camouflage your house doors and windows if not kept under control. I recall a colleague who visited New Zealand for a six week holiday only to return and discover he couldn't find his kitchen door.

If shrubs and trees are planted too close together and they overlap or intertwine, then a life saving dose of pruning will help them survive. Branches that rub together or dead shoots will prove counterproductive and need removing. Dead wood is no longer of any use to the plant and failure to carry out this task will spawn disease. If you are uncertain whether a shoot is dead, try scraping away the bark or cork tissue. If you discover any green underneath, this would tend to suggest it is still alive. Brown or grey colouration means the prognosis is less optimistic and the shoot is likely to be dead.

"Trees for your garden ? – Choose carefully"

If a branch looks deceased, don't snap it off where it joins the main stem because it may still be alive for part of its length. Make your cut where the living tissue finishes and the plant should produce its own callus or seal to prevent entry of disease-causing material. I have witnessed many a pruner using unpleasant vocabulary when they discover they have just removed a perfectly healthy shoot.

Many of us find bramble a problem in our hedges and herbaceous borders. You will decide it's time it needs removing when it lacerates your arms or removes your hat as you walk by. Bramble is a prickly and aggressive shrub and a member of the rose family. If you want rid of this injurious plant, do not try to prune it back. This will increase its determination to cause you even more discomfort. You must dig out the offending weed and ensure its root is totally removed.

Where a plant is grown for its flowers or fruits, the processes that need to occur to produce these structures will consume much energy. Often pruning is necessary to allow the plant to conserve its energy and focus on the flower and fruit production. This can be observed when fruit trees are not pruned and both the quality and number of fruits will be affected. Dead-heading flowers, that is removing old and faded flowers, is a simple form of finger pruning in that it allows energy to be shunted into producing new flowers instead of forming fruits and seeds. However, do not dead-head fruit tree flowers otherwise your tree will not bear fruit and the term, Dead Head, will then be applied to you.

"Wear protective clothing when pruning"

Whenever you decide to make a cut on a branch or shoot you will notice buds along its length. Decide how long you want these shoots to be and then apply your surgery. If these buds seem to alternate along the shoot, make your cut about one quarter of an inch immediately above the bud you have chosen. Try to cut at an angle of about twenty-five degrees, but don't bother borrowing your son's geometry set to verify this. The cut should be made at this angle so that the cut slopes away from the bud. This type of cut is widely practised in pruning, because it is designed to let rainwater run off the cut surface away from the bud while at the same time keeping a reduced surface area, making it difficult for bacteria and fungi to enter.

If you notice the shoot has two buds opposite each other, then again make your cut at about one quarter of an inch above the buds, but this time it should be horizontal. Armed with this fundamental practical knowledge, you can proceed to make more cuts than you would find suggested in a government green paper on defence.

To further complicate pruning matters, but for best results, different plants should be pruned at certain times of the year. Now, to prevent you from throwing this book into the compost heap and adopting the philosophy that to prune plants you need a degree in horticulture, as our Gallic friends would say, 'Restez calme!' The simple advice is shrubs that flower early in the year can be pruned as soon as their flowers fade. Shrubs that flower late in the summer should have their pruning left to the following spring. Fruit trees should always be pruned in winter. There, that wasn't too technical, was it? However, you may be impatient and wish to instantly remedy your overgrown small patch of Britain. You can ignore this guidance and sometimes be fortunate in avoiding disease and growth problems. Best of luck!

Should you inherit or even cause a neglected gardenscape and you wish to improve its appearance, the first task is to look at the plants it contains and attempt to assign them into simple plant groups. There are roughly six plant groups to which each of your garden plants belong - the flowering shrubs, ornamental trees, fruit bushes, climbers, hedges and roses. By doing this you will be able to decide on the type of pruning they need. If this simple classification task gives you problems, then perhaps let someone else help. You may feel happier with the classification that these green objects are simply plants and that diagnosis is the limit of your botanical repertoire.

If you do wish to know individual plant names, a visit to a garden centre or library can be a helpful journey. I would suggest you carefully scrutinize the plant's name and pronounce it correctly. I overheard a confused male gardener telling a group of ladies that his wife has a wonderful clitoris that she has on view in their front garden. Clematis was the plant to which our muddled horticulturalist was referring.

Some fundamental information about these major plant groups, which will help you perform correct basic pruning is set out on the next page:

"Remember you can't glue bits back on"

A) Flowering shrubs – these are woody plants with several branches but no central stem. They may be small, such as heathers or lavenders, or larger examples up to several metres high. Good examples of taller types would include buddleia, the butterfly bush, and berberis, the barberry. Some species of shrub lose their leaves in winter and are called deciduous while others retain their leaves throughout the year, being referred to as evergreen.

Evergreen shrubs are usually pruned to give them shape or to prevent them appearing overcrowded. They are best pruned in late spring and there isn't much chance of doing much harm to them if your pruning is light.

The rest of your garden shrub-pruning programme is geared by the seasons and the time of the year they flower. Shrubs that flower early in the year from spring to mid-summer include many garden favourites, such as wiegela, lilacs and forsythia. They should be pruned as soon as their flowers fade. Your pruning duty here is to ensure that the plant's energy resources are used to produce new healthy shoots for the following year that will once more bear flowers. Again, if it is shape or reducing congestion you set out to achieve, reduce the length of their shoots but leave the shoot with some buds from which fresh growth can occur.

Late summer-flowering shrubs complete their flowering cycle by late September and their pruning should be left until late spring. This management prevents any new-formed tender shoots being ripped apart by frosts over the winter.

Winter flowering shrubs are easy to manage. As soon as flowering is complete, usually by the end of March, prune any dead stems and give the plant fresh shape. Also remove any congested growth to prevent air stagnancy developing in the centre of the plant framework, thus preventing disease conditions.

B) Ornamental trees – these include the types of small trees found in many domestic gardens designed to give some height, colour or a focal point. They would include acers (maples), betula (birches), prunus (ornamental cherry) and the fruit trees of apple and pear.

Should you have inherited a specimen tree in your landscape, such as a mature oak, willow or poplar, then I would be careful when it comes to extensive pruning or even its removal. Both of these tasks are best performed by professional tree surgeons because it is a skilled undertaking. It is also wise to check that any specimen tree on which you wish to operate, has no tree preservation order. If this is the case, you should inform the local council arboriculturist before doing anything. I should also point out that removing a large tree which has grown for years close to your house and appears to have caused no problems with your foundations, could possibly cause complications after its removal. This may be due to ground heave because of changes in the water content of the soil.

If you purchase a very young tree from a garden centre, you will have to undertake some formative pruning to give it a shape or an appearance pleasing to the eye for years to come. In its first winter, cut away any shoots that are competing with the main stem. Also ensure no

"Don't take risks when pruning"

branches are rubbing together or overlapping. The following spring, cut away any of the lower branches near the ground to give it a visible trunk. Then reduce by half the shoots in the middle part of the stem for the main trunk to thicken. In the following winter, remove these cut side shoots to give the tree a lollipop appearance. This formative pruning sets the skeleton of the tree from now on and the plant will need little trimming. Should any dead or diseased wood appear, carry out your minimal pruning during the winter months.

Because of their year-round greenery, conifers can be a useful addition to any garden. In general terms they are easy trees to manage and require little pruning, other than ensuring they have a central main stem from which the side growth will develop. Maintain this shape with only very light pruning of these side branches. Dead side shoots appear as brown patches and are unsightly. They will not get better, so remove them. Make your cut deep inside the plant so that the cut will be masked by adjacent foliage. Too many dead, brown branches make the tree look like it has suffered a Napalm attack and the tree will need replacing. Snow can damage young conifers simply because of its weight, and this can upset root anchorage in the soil and also bend shoots. Brush the snow from these conifer branches to prevent such problems. I do, however, remember one former neighbour whose garden resembled the set from 'I'm a celebrity. Get me out of here!' He positively welcomed snowfalls because he would say that now his garden looked exactly like mine.

Some trees and flowering shrubs produce suckers (new shoots) away from the base of the main stems. This new

growth is unwanted, because it saps the strength of the
parent plant and they will soon take over. It's best to do
a Humphrey Bogart impression as you snip them away
and say, 'So long, suckers!'

Two of the most commonly grown fruit trees in domestic
gardens are apples and pears. Should your tree or bush
look overgrown and out of control then, if possible, you
need to establish a basic framework of branches from
which your fruiting side shoots will develop. If your
neighbours call your tree Boots the Chemists, because it
seems to have branches everywhere, try to produce a
main stem about 75cm high with three to four side
branches radiating out from it. This may appear radical
pruning. However, within a couple of seasons this
structure will have grown between eight to ten smaller
side branches (laterals) and an open centre. Such a typical
fruit tree skeleton will allow ease of fruit picking and
prove uncomplicated to maintain. Also in winter, when
the tree is dormant, cut back the end third of each leader
branch and reduce the numbers of buds to five on each
side shoot. This will improve the quality of the fruit you
will pick the following summer.

C) Roses – It seems incredible that a rose flower with
its beautiful fragrant petals can arise from thorny
shoots capable of inducing pain, haemorrhage and
possible blood poisoning. Whenever you tackle some
serious pruning of roses, always take care and wear
thick gloves and never a short-sleeved shirt. Also,
gather all clippings when your pruning session is
complete, because rose thorns do not respect tyres, feet
or footballs.

For many there seems to be a mystique about pruning roses and you will discover textbooks devoted to rose management. Roses are classified as to the way they grow and flower. Floribunda roses are bush roses with dense clusters of semi and double blooms. Hybrid tea roses are again bush roses, but with large blooms fewer in number than the floribundas. Climbing roses form a permanent framework that will grow up a trellis, pergola or wall. Their side shoots produce an abundance of colourful blooms. However, they are not self-supporting and must be given some structure on which they can be tied. Rambling roses are best avoided in small domestic gardens because, as their name suggests, they get everywhere and their long, whippy shoots possess thousands of large thorns. So, unless you are into masochism, acupuncture or becoming a blood donor, these types are best omitted from your garden scheme.

In an attempt to cut through (apologies for the pun) the theory of pruning roses, the following basic information should help. Dead-head all roses on a weekly basis to promote fresh blooms and new shoots. If you have large flowered or cluster flowered roses, shorten their main stems by half and any side shoots to two buds. Any roses showing dead or dying shoots should be cut back to healthy buds. If you have inherited a climbing rose, shorten the flowering side shoots to two or three buds. Always tackle rose pruning in early spring before the buds burst open. In the autumn, shorten extra long stems of bush roses and remember to make your cuts 6cm above a bud at a slight slope.

D) Climbers – I recall purchasing my first climber from a garden centre and then upsetting my wife by immediately cutting it back by one half. She assured me I should be sectioned under the Mental Health Act and refused to accept my explanation that the purpose of doing this was to allow fresh growth from near the base. I further failed to secure Brownie points when she saw me cut away all but four of these new strong stems which she had carefully tied to the trellis. Again, my explanation was to stimulate further stronger growth for the next flowering season. Her silent yet effective response meant I had to tread very carefully over the next few days.

Climbers will sometimes support themselves by either twining around supports in a way similar to runner beans, or by gripping onto supporting walls by suckers or adventitious roots. The former will include the fragrant honeysuckle and wisteria, whereas ivy and the Virginia creeper bear aerial roots.

Some climbers produce small stalks, called tendrils, that do the climbing and provide anchorage. Sweet peas and cucumbers also have these supportive structures, but in many domestic gardens you will see them on clematis, passion flowers and vines. The aggressive Russian vine is worth a mention here. I think it best to avoid the latter, because it will take over not only your wall space but the rest of the houses in your road too!

If you have left your climber unchecked for years, you can still rejuvenate it; though this may also take a couple of years. You will, of course, see a mass of tangled and twisted woody stems and you will scratch your head knowing where to start. The initial thing to do is to give the plant a good watering, feed and then a thorough haircut. This prescription will immediately help invigorate anything or anyone down on their luck. Cut out dead and diseased shoots. Cut them back to healthy-looking buds and slowly, over a few seasons, cut out about a third of older stems. Maintain the watering and feeding programmes and you will be pleasantly surprised with the results.

The most common climber in gardens is clematis. How they are pruned depends upon when they flower. Ones that flower in late summer and into autumn can be cut right down to ground level at the end of summer. Varieties that flower early in the season before mid-summer should be pruned immediately after flowering. Do this by reducing the side shoots to within three or four buds of the main skeleton. In general, varieties that flower from mid-winter to late spring should not need much pruning on an annual basis, but if they do appear overgrown after some years of growth, cut out over-vigorous shoots and trim the plant to contain it.

Climbers are effective members of any garden because they can camouflage bare walls, hide unsightly objects such as oil tanks, dustbins and nosey neighbours. Their vertical growth they provide allows a new and colourful dimension to your garden.

E) Fruit bushes – the principal soft fruit bushes you may have in your garden or allotment will probably be raspberries and gooseberries. Raspberries are known as

"Step back frequently to check your progress"

cane fruits because they are borne on vertically-trained woody canes. There are two types, the autumn and summer varieties. Autumn fruiting raspberries bear their fruit in the autumn on new shoots formed this year. They are easy to manage. When they have finished yielding their crop and when winter comes, cut these canes down to three inches from the ground. The next growing season will see new shoots push through and eventually produce fresh fruit in September.

Summer fruiting raspberries produce their fruits on last year's canes and the best time to prune them is immediately after you have harvested their fruit. Any canes that have borne fruit must be cut back to ground level because they will not fruit again. That is why it is best to prune after gathering all of the fruit as you can easily tell old from new canes. Your job now is to tie in the new, fresh canes that will produce next year's crop. Leave one cane for every 10cm and avoid overcrowding. When they have reached the top wire of your support, remove their tips. Beware leaving suckers on these plants; they sap the strength of your fruiting canes and often come up in the garden next door.

Gooseberries are borne on bushes that are best pruned to give a wine glass shape or framework. This is achieved early on by some formative pruning. You should aim for a bush containing a short central stem with about five side shoots. If you prune these shoots each down to about three buds, this provides the basic bush shape. Remember this pruning channels fresh energy into fruit formation and is also designed to make fruit picking easier. Beware of some gooseberry bush spines, they can be vicious!

F) Hedges – these structures provide screens, partitions and boundaries in a garden. My teenage son's double entendre in his GCSE Geography examination also reflects yet another practical use of hedges. He wrote,

'Hedgerows help farmers to break wind in their fields.'

The hedges that typify many of our gardens will include conifer, beech, hawthorn, laurel and privet. Formal hedges should be clipped regularly to maintain a bushy and neat appearance and, with the exception of laurel, most can be trimmed with shears or hedgecutters to maintain shape. Laurel shoots are best shortened with secateurs to avoid ripping the leaves.

Conifer hedges make excellent quick-growing hedges, but they too require regular pruning to maintain their size. If you fail to do this, they will grow far too wide and tall and look atrocious when you try restorative pruning. Conifers do not grow well from old wood, so little and often in the growing seasons is the magic formula. I prefer conifer hedges pruned with a sloping cut so that the top is narrower than the bottom. This allows sun and air to reach all parts of the hedge, ensuring that the foliage remains a uniform healthy colour.

Beech hedges for me are the quintessential British garden hedge. Their beautiful summer foliage is maintained during autumn and winter as copper vestiges. Most beech hedges need only be pruned once a year.

The Ten Commandments of Pruning

1. Pruning is performed to achieve shape, health, good flowers and fruits.

2. If in doubt, always prune too little rather than too much. You cannot stick back on pieces that you have cut.

3. Remove branches that are dead, crossed or are rubbing together.

4. Any cuts you make should be about one-quarter of an inch above a bud at some twenty-five degree angle. For buds that are opposite each other, your cut should be horizontal, again at about a quarter of an inch above these buds.

5. A shoot will continue growing straight unless you remove its tip. When this bud tip is removed, side shoots appear, growing from buds below the cut. This will eventually make the stem look branched and bushy.

6. Dead-head flowers to maintain and improve flowering.

7. Always wear appropriate clothing when pruning roses, brambles and other thorny bushes.

8. Always use the correct equipment to match your pruning activities. Secateurs should give a clean cut and not tear the branch. If it does this, you should be using loppers.

9. If you are uncertain whether a shoot is dead, scrape the wood or bark away to check for any sign of green or white colouration.

10. Always stand on the ground to prune plants. Do not balance on shaky ladders or boxes.

5

GROWING YOUR OWN VEGETABLES

It is absolutely true. There's nothing like the taste of fresh vegetables, cooked only minutes after they have been picked from your garden. Another bonus is the fact that you know how these vegetables have been grown and what has been put on them. If you do have enough ground space to devote to 'growing your own', there is no end to the range of vegetables you can produce throughout the year. The majority of us will, of course, need to be selective with our crops and only choose those we like and types that do not take up too much space. Small patches will not support many plants the size of sweetcorn or courgettes. These consumables require extensive areas with precious little room for anything else. A modest sized plot will, however, support lettuce, radishes, carrots, French and runner beans, beetroot and spring onions, leaving some room for a row of new potatoes.

The first important issue when contemplating growing vegetables is that the ground must be suitable to support these crops. You will easily tell the quality and type of your soil by digging a couple of spadefuls and feeling the texture of this soil sample. Please do not stop reading at

"There is nothing better than growing your own"

this point. I am aware I have used the term 'digging', this word should not induce sweating, palpitations and a desire to now purchase your veg from the local supermarket.

Heavy soils, typified by clay, are hard to dig and knock over. They are cold and wet but have plenty of mineral salts in them. Sandy, light soils, on the other hand, are very easy to dig and they warm quickly but lack mineral salts because of their quick drainage. You should try to engineer a loam soil with the good characteristics of both clay and sand, together with a generous amount of humus. For those readers who are a dab hand with sandwiches, humus is not the paste you spread on pitta bread. You are confusing this with the homonym, humous. Horticultural humus is decomposing animal and plant material and can come in many forms, from horse manure to mushroom compost. Most economical gardeners use the rotted components of their compost heaps. Leaf litter that has rotted down also gives excellent results. Humus gives soils a better structure and food holding capacity. Nevertheless, if someone recommends you putting pig manure on your rhubarb, I would oppose their suggestion and stick to custard.

The part of vegetable growing that novice gardeners do not find appealing is preparing the ground. Digging shouldn't be hard work. The trick is not to turn over too big a section of ground, and also not to dig huge chunks of earth each time you insert the spade. This is particularly important when digging clay soils. The spade should be inserted into the soil at right angles to the ground, to a spade blade depth or 'spit'. If you are preparing your new ground in the autumn or winter, remove the weeds as you move along; but don't bother breaking up the earth. Leave it as big chunks for the frost to attack. You will see that in the spring time the soil will then break open easily. As you dig, throw in some manure or composted material.

Do not be tempted to dig too deeply. The moment you start bringing to the surface the parent rock, Satan or perhaps a kangaroo, you have obviously overdone it. The majority of vegetables root and grow happily in about nine inches of soil.

Many people with small vegetable plots nowadays have gone over to raised beds. These are usually 4ft wide patches of ground, kept in place by a border of some description. This allows you to improve the quality of this potential growing area, because the drainage is improved and the soil will be warmer. They are particularly useful in parts of the country whose parent soil is clay. I use old scaffold boards as soil retainers. They allow me to build up a volume of good soil which will never compact, because the narrowness of each bed means you do not need to tread on this ground when you plant or hoe. Do not be tempted to use railway sleepers to construct raised beds for growing vegetables. They may look neat and rustic but they will slowly leach their preservatives and contaminate your soil. It is easy to construct a small, portable wooden bridge that will span this raised bed if you find accessing the middle of the bed difficult. However, this structure may prove challenging to use if you suffer from vertigo or alcoholism.

"Don't dig too deep"

Once the task of preparing your plot is complete, keeping it looking good and in shape requires little attention. Take out the weeds with a hoe as they appear.

If your intended vegetable plot is choked with weeds and grasses and you are allergic to the digging process required to remove this greenery, then you can use a weed killer containing glyphosate. This is a systemic herbicide (a chemical which penetrates the leaves of the weed and slowly journeys through the plant to the roots, killing the plant tissue). Follow the dosage application on the product label and, depending on the weather conditions, your soil will be ready for turning over within a couple of weeks. Glyphosate products biodegrade into non-toxic compounds after they have acted, and are not supposed to harm your soil. If you water or spray the product onto this weed-festooned area, then follow safety instructions and use a mask, gloves and eye protection. Remember to avoid spraying adjacent areas that are weed free and contain your specimen plants.

Should even the thought of digging lead to apoplexy, you may wish to purchase a small tiller to help you turn over your soil. There are some lightweight models on the market. I purchased one when my cardiovascular system started to remind me that I was not in my forties any more. I find them extremely useful for aerating the soil, mixing in compost and breaking the soil down to a fine tilth. They can even take the hard work out of digging a trench for planting potatoes. However, there are small tillers and ones the size of a Challenger tank. The latter are only useful if you have an urge to rotivate the whole of Denmark. Choose a model that is easily carried and manoeuvrable. It is also important that you don't need a degree in mechanical engineering to start it. A gentleman who had an allotment not far from my own, possessed a cumbersome contraption that would shower everyone with black smoke each time he used it. It was made in Germany and was quite a formidable beast that he called A Tiller the Hun. Get it?

Whenever crops grow, they take nutrients out of the soil. Manuring will replace some of these essential plant requirements and you may be tempted to use a fertilizer to enrich this growing patch. Choose a fertilizer that suits your soil. All shop-bought fertilizers will list the percentage of nitrogen, phosphate and potassium they contain. It is referred to as the NPK rating, with the 'K' cipher referring to potassium. In general, N for nitrogen (nitrate) is the leaf maker, P for phosphate is the root maker, and potassium is the flower and fruit maker. From this you can understand why tomato fertilizers are rich in potassium salts, and fertilizers - designed to bring on any of the brassicas (cabbage family members) - will contain plenty of nitrogen.

I believe the older types are still fairly cheap and give excellent results. Fish, Blood and Bone may sound like the name of a boy band, but it is a slow-release organic fertilizer and supplies all of the nitrogen, potash and phosphate your plants will need. This substance has a powerful smell. I am of the opinion that anything smelling as pungent as that, must be good. It certainly clears my sinuses.

"Some rotovators are too big for the job"

"Fish blood and bone certainly clear your sinuses"

Growmore, too, has been used for years and has immense popularity as an artificial balanced fertilizer in that it always yields quality growth, when used correctly. There are many other fertilizers that exist as 'compounds' or 'straights'. 'Compounds' give a broad spectrum of mineral salt release, whereas 'straights' target and remedy the lack of a specific commodity such as iron or magnesium. Sequestered iron and Epsom Salts respectively are typical examples.

Whichever brand you choose, remember not to overfeed as this may scorch the roots. Always follow safety precautions in terms of eye protection, mask and gloves. Mineral nutrients are taken up by plant roots in solution and so their effects are frequently witnessed after it has rained. If it hasn't rained for some time, get out the hosepipe and water in the fertilizer. I'm a great believer in rainwater itself acting as a nitrogen feed. It's quite amazing how healthy and invigorated your produce will look after a spell of rain. Saving water in water butts and using this source from the watering can is just as effective, as long as it has not been allowed to stagnate.

Some vegetable plants respond well to an occasional foliar feed. This is when the leaves of the plants are watered with your fertilizer solution. Brassicas and tomato plants love an occasional foliar feed, but need to draw their nutrients principally from the soil.

When all of your winter digging is done, there's nothing better than to plan the vegetables you intend to grow and then to order your seeds. If you have never grown edible produce before, I would advise you to keep your selection as simple as possible in order to guarantee good results. The list of crops mentioned at the beginning of the chapter is a good starting point. Seeds can be purchased from garden centres or you can send away for seed catalogues and order from them. Each seed packet will tell you when and how to sow the seeds. Most vegetable seeds can be sown straight into the ground, but you will produce excellent transplantable young plants when you sow into plug modules. I would advise buying some of these modules from a garden centre and, if you look after them, they will last many growing seasons. The logic behind these containers is that you sow the seeds directly into compost within these cells. The young plantlets will develop, enabling you to push or squeeze them out and plant them directly into the soil. In doing this, you do not disturb the roots. They do not miss the move and become established in the soil quicker. Try sowing two or three seeds per module to allow for poor germination and then pull out or 'thin' the ones you do not want.

Make a plan of your plot and decide where you will grow your vegetables. Make a note of anything that may affect the growth and development of your plants. Hedges, trees or garden buildings may cast shade at different times of the year. Growing plants near a hedge can significantly reduce their cropping potential since the roots of the hedge will draw many nutrients and much of the water. The tall hedge will also reduce the amount of light reaching them. Keep a copy of your plan for next year. This will allow you to practise the essential principle of crop rotation. In simple terms this means not growing plants in the same place year after year. This technique avoids the build-up of certain soil-living pests which target specific crops. It also guards against the soil becoming empty of certain mineral salt nutrients. There is a standard formula for dividing your vegetable plot into thirds and planting ROOTS, BRASSICAS and OTHERS one year, and then changing each sector the next by moving each type forward. The science is to follow a three-year rotational plan. If you want an easier life, simply make a note of not growing the same thing in the same place every year. This procedure works just as well and becomes less like solving a giant sudoku.

Seeds need water, warmth and air to germinate. To complete the germination process, they will also require light. Keeping your seed trays or modules in a warm place will promote this germination process, but keep checking on them otherwise you will often overcook them and they will dry out. Your courgettes and sweetcorn have to germinate first before you barbeque them.

If you don't expose them to light once they start to germinate, you will cause them to etiolate, which in simple terms means they grow tall, spindly, colourless and lie on the ground exhausted. Such behaviour may remind you of your adolescent son.

You can cover the seed trays or plug modules with a sheet of glass or plastic. Cover this, in turn, with a sheet of newspaper but check for growth on a daily basis.

Plants that transplant well from modules into the soil will include lettuce, leeks, tomatoes and any of the brassicas (members of the cabbage family). Sow seeds of the bean family, such as runner beans and French beans, straight into small three-inch pots and then move them directly into the soil.

Root vegetables, such as parsnips, beetroot and carrots, do not transplant well as they do not like their roots disturbed. However, I have seen some impressive results by them being carefully removed from modules with plenty of soil around their roots. The amateur should really sow straight into the ground.

One common mistake made when sowing seeds is to sow them too deeply. If it says on the packet to cover the seeds with three millimetres of soil, it means cover them with three millimetres (one eighth of an inch) and not three inches of soil. Otherwise the seeds will germinate but die before their tiny shoots can reach the surface. If it says to gently firm the soil over the seeds, then do not thump the soil senseless. Remember, these tiny units of life want as easy a time as possible as they push towards the light.

Sowing seeds in drills means excavating a tiny furrow with the tip of a bamboo cane or the end of your dibber. The drill is a straight line across your plot. Mark the position of this drill with a garden line then start excavating. Carrot and beetroot seeds germinate very well with a fine tilth of soil over the top of them. If your soil still remains in clods, either use sand or some multi-purpose compost to cover them. Try to imagine that each seed will become a carrot and give it the space it needs. Some people over-sow to allow for poor germination and thin out the seedlings once they have germinated.

Failure to do this will result in overcrowding and eventually produce tiny carrots with not enough roots to feed a microscopic rabbit.

Most beetroot seeds are, in fact, clusters of seeds stuck together. Therefore, you are more than justified to sow them thinly otherwise you will finish up with all leaf and no root.

With the drill now complete and covered with fine soil, mark the position of this seedbed with a stick so that you know where it is. There is nothing worse than looking at a patch of ground and scratching your head trying to remember what and where you placed your seed. In my youth, I remember lovingly watering a group of creeping buttercup some feet away from where I had sown a row of carrots. Many gardeners push the seed packet over the top of this marking stick. High winds and torrential rain can often remove the identities of these packets, which results in a state of confusion. I suggest using an indelible marking pen to write on a stick the name and date of the seed sown.

Some vegetable seeds such as parsnip are very light in weight. I would not advise you sowing them into prepared seed drills on a windy day, otherwise you may find them germinating in next door's garden.

Most vegetable seeds will not germinate at temperatures below seven degrees Celsius. If you warm the ground before and after sowing your seeds, this will increase their germination. This can be achieved by spreading a sheet of transparent polythene over the area where you wish to grow your plants. Such practice is particularly helpful in the early parts of the year when the ground may still be cold and very wet. Even better is if you make a cloche and place this contraption over the growing area. Cloches come in all shapes and sizes and they do extend your growing season. Some people use panes of glass angled together across their plot and the end product resembles a giant, transparent Toblerone. The problem with these structures is that should they ever shatter, thanks to an over-zealous teenage catapulter or high winds, then the resulting small pieces of glass can often take ages to find. Plastic sheets or clear polythene are ideal. Old metal coat hangers can easily be moulded and shaped into hoops, across which you can hang this polythene. Many allotmenters now use the blue, flexible plastic water pipes as arches for their polythene cloches.

Something that can be extremely frustrating about growing your own is a rash of late frosts in spring. Your potatoes or tender lettuce may be looking good, only to be threatened by a couple of nights of ground frosts. There is no need for you to panic and light a bonfire nearby, nor is it necessary for you to play a blowlamp near them at three o'clock in the morning. Horticultural fleece is your lifesaver. If you purchase a small roll of this material and look after it, it will last you years. Cover your row of prize vegetables with this fleece and it will prevent the leaves burning from frost action. Should the weather take a sudden cold turn and you are caught short up the garden, then a couple of sheets of newspaper will prove helpful, though toilet roll is more hygienic. Newspaper acts as a night-time insulating layer when laid over your tender crop, even if you are not taken short.

A popular medium used for rearing tomatoes, peppers and vegetables is the growbag. Their potential to grow a wide repertoire of crops makes them an asset to any household, particularly useful if you lack space and want to grow your produce on a patio. I believe you can grow any vegetables in growbags. Admittedly, you will have to choose a short rooting variety of carrots and parsnips, but go for it! I have even seen people have success with sweetcorn raised in growbags, but in terms of tending time and product return I would not recommend this method.

Growbags do vary in price and quality. As their compost becomes hydrated, their bulk will increase. However, some of the cheaper varieties do contain less growing medium and this factor will limit tap root growth. A tap root is the main or central root, which in root vegetables is the structure containing the stored nutrients we will eat. Non-root vegetables or fruits, such as tomatoes, peppers and cucumbers, will spread their roots sideways and fill all parts of the growbag. Experiment with different examples until you discover the one you feel gives best results. Remember, you will be able to purchase peat or peat-free growbags and, once again, that's your choice.

There is, however, an imperative for growbag success. Never let them dry out. This is easily done, particularly at the end of a hot summer's day. Peat-based growing media can dry out and are very difficult to completely rehydrate. Erratic watering can lead to all sorts of problems with tomatoes. If you can use a hose then do so, and spend some time slowly filling each bag. Stick your fingers into the bag after your watering efforts and check the compost mixture is thoroughly sodden. There should already be drainage holes in the under surface or sides of the bag. If you discover there are not, make a couple with your garden knife.

As you become familiar with growbag use, you will know when to start feeding. I have used some anaemic bags over the years that contain few nutrients and demand feeding almost immediately. This is not good and this type of bag will certainly affect your fruit or vegetable returns. It does not always follow that the more expensive the bag, the better will be your results. Again, shop around and try a few experiments.

Runner beans will grow happily in growbags as long as you allow the shoots to climb up a plastic mesh or some canes. One common mistake is to let the base of the shoots blow around and this will disturb the roots due to a tugging effect caused by wind. French beans will grow happily in two litre pots. One plant of Canadian Wonder French bean will readily fill such a pot and give you enough pods for a family meal. The beauty of French beans is that they continue cropping and, if you stagger your sowing, you secure a continuous supply, some of which can be frozen. Beans always do well in the open soil too. If you are adventurous, try some different kinds, from the pencil-podded varieties to the colourful Borlotti types.

In terms of looking after your vegetables, remember to water them regularly. Reduce competition for nutrients by removing weeds. If you have a small vegetable plot, the hoe should take care of these intruders. Hoeing in the early part of the day means that if you can't be bothered to pick up the weeds, then the drying action of the sun will finish them off by the end of the day. Most vegetable plants will not need feeding once they are growing. They will receive their NPK from the fertilizer you have already worked into the soil. An exception to this, however, is for over-wintered spring greens. They seem to benefit from a nitrogen feed in early spring.

The Ten Commandments for Growing Your Own Vegetables

1. Know the type of soil you have, eg. clay, sandy, stony, etc, and do something about improving its quality.
2. Digging doesn't have to be hard work. Choose a day when the soil has dried and turns over well. Never dig when it's too wet.
3. Don't try to dig too deeply or cover a large area. Little and often is again the prescription.
4. Remove weeds by hand as you dig or spray the area with glyphosate well in advance of your digging programme.
5. Add manure, rotted compost and leaf mould to improve the organic content of your soil and throw in some long-acting organic fertilizer.
6. Choose the vegetables you want to grow and draw up a plan of the plot as well as a seed-sowing or planting calendar. Follow instructions on the seed packets.
7. Try growing some of your vegetables in small modules to give them a good start. Plant out these plug plants when the conditions are right.

8. Never sow seeds too thickly and be prepared to thin them out if they are sown directly into the ground.
9. Use cloches to protect your plants from the wind and cold. They extend your growing season.
10. Practise some form of simple crop rotation to ensure healthy plant growth each year.

6

GARDEN PESTS AND DISEASES

My interpretation of the term pest is any animal or plant you do not wish to be in your garden. This will embrace a wide range of organisms from greenfly to next door's cat. I also include weeds as garden pests simply because they too are unwanted members and will frequently out-compete the plants we do want to fill our garden space. Unfortunately on occasions, I suppose I should include children in this category. Pests can devastate your garden very quickly. Kids playing football against your beautiful herbaceous borders can produce similar destruction with even greater rapidity.

Whether you have a small back garden or several acres of land, pests will always be a problem. Even Essex farmers are plagued with unwanted pests that attack their cereal crops. These pests wear baseball caps, trainers and use mobile phones. So, as the Bible proposes, they must separate the wheat from the Chavs.

The most common animal garden pests include slugs and snails, aphids, vine weevils, caterpillars, mice and rats, moles, birds and badgers. On occasions it is sometimes difficult to decide whether or not an insect you find close

"Garden pests get everywhere"

to your half-eaten dahlias is responsible for such an assault. I have heard gardeners employ a fundamental, if erroneous, rule for judging friend or foe:

'If it quickly scurries away it is a friend. If it moves slowly or not at all then it will fall into the pest category.'

Classic examples of the latter will include slugs, snails, greenfly, woodlice and caterpillars. The dreaded vine weevil adult will even play dead when you shake it from a half-munched rhododendron leaf. I remain unconvinced about the first part of this garden folklore. Badgers leg it with tremendous acceleration when you come across them devouring your three rows of prize sweetcorn. Moles can also achieve Formula One speeds when you have missed them with your garden spade trying to protect your newly-planted runner beans. Ladybirds, on the other hand, are slow movers but are one of the gardener's strongest allies.

When a pest becomes a serious problem, there is a tendency to search for some chemical agent to solve your misfortune. Chemicals can often provide the quick fix. However, I would suggest that even the least eco-friendly of us should take some responsibility for our planet and see if there is an alternative method for dealing with the problem. In agriculture there exists a synergy between chemical and biological means for controlling pests and the diseases they can cause. It is called an integrated form of pest management. I feel that even in our own garden micro-experience there should be a place for controlling many pests by non-chemical means. Biological control frequently involves the use of predators to consume the pest. Documented examples of this practice include using toads and hedgehogs to eat slugs. Lacewings and ladybirds voraciously devour aphids. Many people do not care for spiders. They also help to reduce insect pests. I never intentionally remove their webs from inside my polytunnel. However, I often emerge from this structure looking like Miss Haversham from '*Great Expectations*' after a spell of tomato picking in the summer.

Garden slugs and snails have gained a lot of bad press over their millions of years of evolution, because they are true herbivores. For non-scientists, a herbivore is an organism that eats many forms of plant life and not just herbs. These slimy, seemingly lethargic gastropods are far from lazy in that they can devastate garden shrubs, bedding plants and vegetables in a few hours. Where you will find one slug, you will almost certainly discover others. They hunt in packs and can destroy a mature hosta in a couple of hours. If you discover and kill a battalion of these creatures during your seek and destroy mission, do not think the battle is over. It is almost like the film 'Zulu' in that the next evening there will be another wave of them ready for more action.

The most widely used chemical agent for killing slugs and snails is slug pellets. These vary in their efficacy. They must, however, be used in accordance with the concentration recommended on the packaging. Most pellets are supposed to biodegrade if they are not consumed. Another negative about the use of slug pellets is their ability to be consumed by small mammals, birds and little children. Despite safe and green proclamations, I continue not to be a fan of these agents.

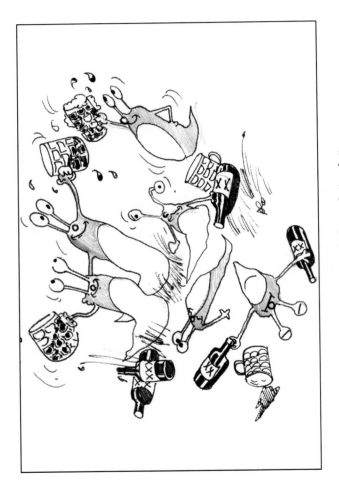

"Slugs and snails love their ale"

Slugs and snails tend to feed at night and so if you want to patrol your lettuce and petunias before midnight, armed with a bucket, then you will collect scores of these itinerants. Pouring salt on a slug will certainly kill it but this method is, I feel, reserved for psychopaths. It is a waste of salt and will prove an unpalatable over-seasoned snack for any hungry hedgehog, as well as giving them high blood pressure.

Slug pubs are extremely effective devices for killing slugs. A yoghurt pot filled with beer and sunk into the soil will catch and destroy many of these pernicious garden pests. I have found beer to be most effective. Slugs do not appear to have a penchant for lager. In the gastropod world there is no such thing as a lager lout. It is the beer's smell which attracts them. Once reaching the sunken pot, they simply topple into the elixir and drown. What a way to go! I heard tell of one contented dipsomaniac slug surfacing four times full of smiles, before he finally drowned. Place a row of these pots close to the plants you wish to protect.

Slugs and snails also dislike their underparts being irritated. So do I. They do not like crawling over gravel, rough bark and crushed egg shells. I know of one gardener who puts a collar of roofing felt around his cabbages to protect them from these beasts. The rough surface of the felt, plus its tar-like odour, are not to their liking.

Another substance of which they disapprove is soot. It really works well but unfortunately you can't find much around these days. Copper bands, purchased from garden centres and placed around your prized plant specimens, are also slug deterrents. They work by giving the slug a small electric shock generated as its slime reacts with the copper.

Horse hair, too, when placed around your vulnerable plants, is most effective in repelling slugs and snails. Once more they do not appear to enjoy the irritation of crossing this material. I can understand why, because I remember my Grandma had a horse hair sofa which would bring my bare legs out in a rash after a few minutes of being seated on it.

One recent form of biological control for slugs and snails is to use parasitic nematode worms. These nematodes are microscopic threadworms that get into the slugs and lay their eggs. Unless you have a small area plagued with these pests, this remedy will work out expensive. You buy the worms contained in granules which you water onto the soil. These remedies are now available at garden centres, but like any form of biological control it can be rather hit and miss.

Aphids are tiny sap-sucking insects, such as greenfly, whitefly and blackfly. Any aphid infestation will bring about poor plant growth. Aphid activity on your tomato plants will reduce the size of your fruits. Blackfly on your runner beans will also lower the crop yield. Greenfly on your roses will impact on flower production and growth. These voracious parasites have tiny, sharp mouthparts similar to a hypodermic needle. They push this into a plant leaf vein or a sappy stem, ultimately providing them with their nourishment. I always know when I have an aphid problem on my tomato plants because ants run up and down the stems. Sap is under pressure and when the greedy aphid receives his generous hit of this juice, the sap is under so much pressure it is forced out of its bottom. Rather disgustingly, the ants are there to collect this sweet anal exudation. I wouldn't like to come back as an ant. Mind you, I continue not to believe in reincarnation and I didn't even when I was a frog.

Many chemical sprays are effective against aphids. Some will kill the insect on contact with the toxin. These agents are, rather unsurprisingly, referred to as contact insecticides. I am no advocate of this type of pesticide. It is very effective but indiscriminate and will kill friendly insects such as bees and lacewings, as well as the insect criminals.

Another type of insecticide is sprayed upon the leaves of the plant where it is absorbed into the sap. The toxin is, therefore, delivered to the insect from the plant via the sap. These sprays are called systemic insecticides. The chemical is supposed to biologically decompose after several days. Once more, if you decide to pursue control by chemical means, then follow the directions on the packet. The problem with aphids, however, is their rapid rate of breeding. When you use this type of spray it will destroy the adults but not their eggs. When these hatch, the toxin will have lost its potency and you will need to apply another dose.

There are greener ways of tackling aphid problems. Aphids appear not to like the odours emitted from certain plants. Lavender grown amongst your roses will deter these pests. Tagetes (a type of marigold) is a

"Be aware of health and safety issues"

powerful deterrent when planted adjacent to your salad crops. The herb basil will also do the trick when grown between your tomato plants. Pyrethrum plants are also aphid unfriendly.

I knew an eccentric gardening wizard who would make up a spray of crushed garlic cloves in water and liberally apply it to his aphid vulnerable plants. He, indeed, had no aphids and quite unsurprisingly, no friends either.

There is a fine woven mesh available that will prevent even tiny aphids from attacking your plants. I use this when I plant my cabbages and other members of the brassica family. It also helps keep at bay the dreaded cabbage white butterflies whose caterpillars look at my Brussel sprouts and then devour them like a teenager would consume a Big Mac.

One final solution to the aphid problem inside greenhouses is to hang yellow sticky traps. Their vivid yellow colour is supposed to attract the tiny flies and they then permanently adhere to the card. One problem I have noticed with this kind of control is that your clothing sticks to these cards if you brush against them. I now have more wool on my aphid traps than on my woolly hat.

The activities of some wandering mammals who decide to 'pop in' to your garden can, on occasions, cause you heartache. Badgers are extremely powerful mammals capable of causing havoc with your domestic greenery. They can dig up shrubs, gouge holes in your lawn and even make huge intrusions into your garden fence.

"Your strawberries are a midnight feast for badgers"

They visit your garden for food, usually worms and slugs. They also have a predilection for vegetable matter such as sweetcorn and strawberries. Badgers are protected species and it is illegal to hunt or kill them. It is also against the law to tamper with their sets. The only solution I have found effective against badgers, and one which meets with the approval of the RSPCA, is to use electric fencing to keep them out of your garden. This method is not designed to grill or defibrillate the badger as he touches the wire. It simply supplies a small and uncomfortable shock to their snouts. It is even more alarming for them in wet conditions.

Badgers are often perceived as cute and cuddly. They are neither of these. They have sharp carnivorous teeth and long claws. They are, however, sensitive to noise. Before I could afford using electric fencing, I would deal with these nocturnal creatures by leaving Talk radio on at night at a low volume down the bottom of the garden. A 2am broadcasted dose of 'my wife doesn't understand me' from a tiresome and pathetic caller seemed to repel these discerning quadrupeds.

I replaced the scarecrow on my vegetable plot last week. My father-in-law was complaining his arms were getting tired. Small birds will decimate your soft fruit bushes, ravage your lettuces and pull up your onion sets. Wood pigeons like the taste of your cabbages and Brussel sprouts. Many French gardeners will shoot these troublesome birds. I have no intention of copying their ways and would not recommend such a dreadful prescription. Birds are good for the garden in that they eat slugs and caterpillars. However, if your soft fruit bushes are in full crop and prove tempting to our feathered allies, then cover them with a net curtain or garden fleece. Put netting around any brassicas you grow. Tie black cotton lines either side and across your young lettuce plants. Birds catch their wings on these unseen barriers and they are spooked. Other remedies include hanging a line of old CDs over your plants, acting as reflectors. These defences catch the light and frighten the birds as they approach your vulnerable plants. I use a chain of old Val Doonican CDs, though why my mother-in-law purchased them as 'easy listening music' beats me.

Old videotape can be effective as a bird deterrent when stretched across plants. Wind causes the tape to hum and birds find this off-putting, similar to my Val Doonican aversion.

If your garden shows signs of an invasion of rats or mice, then you should act promptly. Mice may look sweet and benign but they can inflict lots of damage on germinating seeds and root crops. I recall having four seed trays of bedding plant seedlings gnawed to soil level by these mischievous beasts. The problem with rodents is that should you discover one, there will be others close by. You have the option of using the humane approach by catching these animals in a cage and then releasing them elsewhere. Should you choose to liberate them further up the road, this is an antisocial and unhelpful remedy. They will subsequently invade someone else's garden and you will be passing on the problem. If you must make the rodent-friendly gesture, release the vermin in the countryside well away from civilization.

Traps and baits are the other solutions. Find where these pests are active and apply the bait, but cover it to prevent birds feeding on it. Clear any excess or uneaten bait after it has been effective. I would also advise attaching string to any trap and then tying this string to an anchor point. Rats often catch their tails in these clamps and run off with your £2.50! There are ultrasonic devices available designed to dissuade mice. They seem less suitable for garden use.

Neighbourhood cats may pass through your garden and decide to use it as a permanent latrine. They love freshly-dug and cultivated ground. They are also not immune from using your garden tubs, troughs and even window boxes as places where they can leave faecal messages.

An irate resident once wrote to the council complaining about her problem with the local cat population.

Her communiqué started:

'Dear Councillor Harris,

My front lawn is always covered with cat poo which I find difficult to swallow.'

Some people have strange dietary habits.

Cat pepper dust has some effectiveness, though I use old open teabags as a cheaper disincentive. I know someone who applies muscular ointments such as Deep Heat to the leaves of his plants to tackle his cat problem. Cats don't like the smell of both these agents and do keep away. A more painful mechanism of feline aversion therapy is to push cocktail sticks into your flower tubs and boxes. They will only attempt one sortie into these containers due to the subsequent acupuncture they receive. Poor man's cocktail stick treatments are thorny rose, pyracantha or berberis stems. It may sound a spiteful process, but it is one you will try when you repeatedly become a victim of their colonic activities.

Weeds are sometimes light-heartedly referred to as plants growing in the wrong place. Also, they do not make it easy for us to manage them because they never grow in straight lines. Annual weeds complete their lifecycle from seed to flowering plant in one year. Perennial weeds, however, come back year after year because of their underground roots or shoots capable of surviving very low temperatures.

All weeds have a direct effect on plant growth. They deprive other plants of light, nutrients and water. Annual weeds in your flowerbeds or vegetable plots can easily be dealt with by hoeing. Your intention is to prevent them from flowering and making seeds. Hoeing cuts them off at soil level, so killing the annual weed. Common annual weeds will include chickweed, sun spurge, groundsel and black nightshade.

Perennial weeds need to be dug out from the soil. If you remove their tops, they will grow back. Some aggressive types such as couch grass will re-emerge even if you leave a small part of their underground stems in the soil. Do not be tempted to rotivate a patch of ground infested with perennial weeds such as couch grass, bindweed, dock and horsetail. This will multiply your problem as you cut the roots and stems.

"Does that sign say toilet"

Should you wince at the thought of digging out these often deep-rooted assassins, use a systemic herbicide such as glyphosate. The weed killer 'Roundup' is a fine example. Correct dilution and application will totally remove your problem within a couple of weeks. If you do not like the idea of spraying and you are prepared to wait a long time for your weeds to disappear, then cover your ground with a tarpaulin or black plastic sheet. This is designed to prevent both light and water reaching the weeds. However, such a treatment will take as long as two or more years to work. If you are the unfortunate victim of horsetail, you will never rid yourself of this pernicious perennial using this method.

Some people purchase weed wands to destroy these plant pests. They are flame gun tools and will destroy the visible part of the weed but frequently fail to kill the deep roots of many perennials. They appear to be suitable for dealing with annual weeds. Be careful when using these gas-burning devices. Setting the base of your shed on fire is easily done if this tool is used irresponsibly. I was told of a chap's lack of concentration while using this tool, and he subsequently melted the rubber soles of his flip-flops. A rather painful way of increasing one's carbon footprint, I think.

You may discover something in your flower border you do not recognize. Could it be an expensive garden plant, or possibly a weed? The crazy rule of thumb is for you to give it a slight tug. If it appears to want to stay put, then it is a weed. Should you find the plant volunteers to part company with the soil, then it is

"Weeds and tarpaulins don't mix"

probably a valuable plant. You will then feel such a dimwit for uprooting it.

There are other chemical substances capable of removing your weed problem. However, I would be reluctant to use any of these treatments you may discover lying in your garden shed. They may be out-of-date and now banned from use because of their environmental unfriendliness. Sodium chlorate was, and still is, used as a weed killer. It is very powerful and once more I would avoid this compound and keep to those currently available and which have a good press. You will find suitable agents on the shelves at garden centres.

Whenever you employ any herbicide to kill weeds, always follow the health and safety directions. Take care not to apply these chemicals too close to the plants you wish to keep. Try protecting rows of plants with polythene sheeting. Individual small shrubs can be covered with a plastic bucket or dustbin while spraying. When gardening close to others, it is wise to remember that you too will be branded a pest if you use pesticides insensitively and irresponsibly.

Diseased plants should never be thrown on your compost heap. Fungal spores and plant viruses will not disappear. Weed seeds too can remain dormant for a considerable period. The last thing you want to do is to reintroduce these agents back into your soil the following year. Take such debris to the local tip or burn it. Bonfires, however, can be a sure-fire way of annoying your neighbours. Another good way of annoying your neighbours is to park across their drive.

The Ten Commandments of Disease and Pest Control

1. Do not always reach for a chemical to solve your pest problem.
2. Try biological forms of control and welcome predators such as toads, ladybirds, lacewings and hedgehogs into your garden.
3. If you must use chemical control, then try and integrate this with some biological means.
4. Chemical control can often affect the friendly organisms in your garden, eg, bees and birds and small mammals.
5. Always follow the health and safety directions on the box, can or packet when using pesticides.
6. Remove annual weeds by hand or hoe rather than spraying with a herbicide.
7. Act swiftly against any pest to avoid multiplying the problem.
8. Either dig out troublesome perennial weeds or use a systemic herbicide containing glyphosate.
9. Never hire or buy a rotavator to deal with a large area or perennial weeds.
10. Never use old pesticides or herbicides you may discover in your garage or shed. They may be prohibited for use due to toxicity reasons. Use any pesticide responsibly.

7

WATER GARDENS

A former colleague would always shower me with saliva during a conversation. His constant lack of oral control led the workforce to give him the nickname, 'Water Features'. However, in the gardening world, water features breathe life into a garden rather than spit. Ponds, streams and water sculptures can create atmosphere, character and act as a focal point. They provide a new dimension for your garden room. It can be relaxing to sit outside and hear the slow trickle of water from a small fountain or cascade. This peaceful splashing sound, however, has a diuretic effect on me and forces numerous visits to the loo.

Nowadays there are many types of water features you can choose. Some of these are available as 'off the peg' structures, such as pre-cast ponds, waterfalls and ornate water sculptures. You can also create your own water feature using butyl liners, rocks and electrical pumps.

If you have been branded a reluctant gardener but nevertheless someone with a penchant for something watery on your plot, then it is important to keep it simple and very low maintenance. This concept is easily achieved in all garden spaces. My opinion is that no matter how large or small your garden, if you would like to add a water feature to it then go for it.

There are two important factors you must consider when planning such an undertaking. These are scale and location. Large water features look incongruous in small gardens. A pond and fountain with the dimensions of those found at the Palace of Versailles or a water cascade similar to the Trevi Fountain are both a little over-ambitious and a trifle *recherché* for any domestic garden. The rule should be 'the smaller the garden, then the smaller the water feature'. Keep things in proportion and do not be swayed by those who advocate large is best. Petite structures could be anything from water barrels, glazed or terracotta pots, stone troughs, drilled slate or wall mounted masks and taps. The peaceful flow of water can be achieved by incorporating a small electrical pump. However, some words of caution here. If you are attempting any electrical installation in your garden, it is advisable to employ a qualified electrician.

There is a delightful range of pre-formed water sculptures, all of which are relatively inexpensive and can enhance an area of your garden. If you live in a flat and have a tiny courtyard or balcony, there will be a water feature available to you in proportionate scale.

If your garden space is large enough to accommodate a small pond, the location of this structure is most important. The degree of success you will have with your pond and how it develops and matures, is certainly influenced by its correct position. Always try to site your

"Don't be too ambitious with your
water garden design"

pond in the sunniest part of the garden. Ponds will not give their intended effect if you locate them in a dull or dark corner. Such low light intensity levels and coldness of the water will rule out the growth of colourful plants such as water lilies and marginal plants. It will also do nothing for the animal life that ponds are meant to attract. Fish and frogs are cold-blooded but they should not have to wear overcoats and woolly hats.

Do not place your pond directly under a tree. You will be faced with problems due to leaf fall, berries and resinous debris. This material will sour the water. Remember, water features such as ponds, streams and waterfalls will be high maintenance if you ignore such advice. Try not to put a pond close to the garden fence. This will create access problems when you wish to undertake some pond clearing.

I must add here that I would not advise installing any pond if you have small children. For health and safety reasons, wait until they are older. You can then throw them into the pond when they wake you up at three o'clock in the morning asking for a lift home from a party. Similarly, on the issue of health and safety, you must ask yourself if a pond is a suitable inclusion if you have elderly or disabled family members?

Many ponds are positioned at the lowest point of the garden. This is fine, but your water feature will give you greater pleasure if it is visible from the house or near to the area where you sit outside in the spring and summer months. Raised ponds surrounded by brickwork may be one solution for positioning this construction.

"Garden ponds are sometimes used
for the wrong reasons"

I would always try to visualize your water feature before you go ahead and construct it. This avoids shock and disappointment when it is finally installed. Pre-cast ponds give you a prescribed shape, so try to imagine how it would look in your allocated area. If you wish to design your own pond then the easiest thing to do is to use a garden hosepipe or clothes line to create the shape you feel suitable for your chosen spot. I would avoid tight nooks and crannies. They are both difficult to construct and maintain. Squares, rectangles or smooth curves are the simplest and most effective shapes to choose.

It is also advisable that you check the area where you want to install your pond. Does it have any underground drains or cables? Ignoring such wise words could be extremely costly. Other problems you may encounter could be tree roots. These can affect the depth of your pond. Again, perhaps constructing a raised pond may be the answer here?

Once you have decided upon the shape and dimensions of the pond, you have the unenviable task of digging it out. Do not be of the opinion that your water depth should match that of the Pacific Trench. A bottom depth of no more than 24 to 30 inches will suffice. This provides any fish with deep enough areas to endure a harsh winter and also provides a decent rooting area for any water lily you may wish to include. If a pond is made too shallow, evaporation of water could be a problem in the summer months and force your koi carp to wear sunscreen.

Ponds also look attractive if they are built with a small ledge below the surface. This will enable you to seat some marginal plants around the edge. These plants will have their roots totally submerged in the water but their shoots, leaves and flowers will be exposed.

Once the hard task of digging is completed, the next important thing to do is to ensure it is level. There is nothing worse than having large areas of exposed pond liner at one end and water up to the very edge at the other. If this is the case, you will have constructed a pond with a slope. Insects such as pond skaters will now use water skis and slalom down your watery incline.

Whether you have chosen a pre-formed pond made from either resin bonded glass fibre or moulded plastic, remember you get what you pay for. The latter can be rather flimsy in construction and will have less chance of surviving the course than the more expensive resin/glass fibre alternatives. Both models will have a better chance of lasting many years if they are seated properly. The moulded shape of the pond determines how much soil you must excavate and from where. Keep trying it in and out, but beware of sharp stones, bits of wire, cut roots and flints. These can easily puncture a hole in your pond before you start. I knew someone who inadvertently left his trowel under his plastic pond. The offending object punctured a small hole in the plastic, causing it to leak as soon as he filled it with water. Whether you are using a preformed pond or a butyl liner, cover the excavated area with two inches of sand, or use liner quilt. This prevents any stones or other sharp objects cutting into your pond wall when it has to bear the weight of the water. Old carpet can be used instead of sand or lining underlay. Both Spanish and Mexican pond constructors openly recommend the use of a quilt-lining material and are often heard shouting, 'Underlay! Underlay!'

If you have decided to go for butyl, you can choose from a range of thicknesses. The thickness usually determines its longevity and durability. The biggest mistake made is not buying enough of this material. Liner has to take up the shape of the dimensions of the hollow you have created. The length of liner needed will be equivalent to the length of your pond plus twice its maximum depth. Its width should be the pond's maximum width plus twice its maximum depth. An example of this calculation would be:

Pond length	Pond width	Maximum
2m	1.5m	depth 1m

Length of liner needed = pond length plus twice maximum depth

$$= 2m + 2 \times 1m$$
$$= 4m$$

Width of liner needed = pond width plus twice maximum depth

$$= 1.5m + 2 \times 1m$$
$$= 3.5m$$

Although this is a textbook calculation, you will discover that pond liner is available in certain lengths and widths and you will often be left with spare. However, it is best to slightly over-estimate. There is nothing worse than being short of liner at the margins.

When you want to seat the butyl in the pond, carefully spread the liner over its outline and then slowly fill the liner with water from a hosepipe. You will now find the liner will sink and mould to the excavated contours. I would not recommend walking over this submerged liner because this may damage the cushion you have established underneath. This is particularly important if you have used an off-the-peg plastic pond. The pressure exerted from your body weight over small areas will be enough for it to crack. Not good for the swear box.

Your final duty is to trim away any excess liner and then to think about hiding these cut margins. Most people use slabs or flat stones. Paving is good if you have created a marginal ledge. The slabs slightly overhang the margins and conceal the liner. It is very important that you cement these slabs in place and make sure they will not move. People have a tendency to stand on them to view the contents of your pond. While you may wish to welcome animal life into your pool, I would suggest a partly-submerged Uncle Stan is not a desirable inclusion.

If you have designed your pond with gently sloping sides, it is easy to use pebbles or small stones to mask the borders of the liner. Make sure these cobbles or stones are washed thoroughly. I would avoid chippings such as Cotswold stone as they slowly release a cloudy sediment into the water and also become coated with algae, which is impossible to remove.

I am not a fan of concrete ponds. Unless these structures are built by someone who works with sand and cement on a regular basis, they are fraught with problems. Land heave or shrinkage, together with frost action, can produce cracks in the concrete skeleton. If you must use

"An alternative way of increasing your pond life"

such material in building a raised pond, I would always advise including a liner as well.

One pleasurable duty is to plant up your pond. I would keep it very simple. Your small pond will accommodate one water lily. Do not purchase one that is regarded as vigorous. It will take over your water and prevent any light reaching the submerged plants. Your water garden centre should be able to advise you on colour, vigour and planting depth. Water lilies do not like to be placed in the middle of flowing water. They will accept a dousing from a small fountain, but will vote against turbulence from any waterfall or cascade. You may want to put in another surface dweller. Beware of duckweed! It will take over the water surface within days and trying to remove it is an impossible task. The spider-like water soldier or the water hyacinth can be alternatives, but they too need careful scrutiny. A variety of marginal plants can be bought from garden centres. They are usually sold in plastic cages and ready for seating on the marginal shelves. Do not overdo it, otherwise you will end up with more plants than water. Some tall yellow flag iris, together with some marsh marigold and miniature bulrush, are colourful inclusions.

Your aim should be to cover half to two-thirds of the water surface with broad, flat lily leaves and other floating plants.. This should prevent the build-up of algae. Algae are tiny green plants that love both light and nutrients. Most ponds suffer from green water until they establish themselves. The key to avoiding a plague of this pea soup, is planting and patience. Place clumps of oxygenating pondweed, such as hornwort or Canadian pondweed, on the floor of the pool. This important team of plants will not only provide oxygen for the water but will help consume excess nutrients. An alternative way of rapidly introducing oxygen into the water is to throw next door's troublesome cat into your pond. Its violent thrashing movements will create thousands of air bubbles.

By starving the algae of light, using leafy surface plants and limiting their supply of nutrients, your green water should soon disappear. If you are constantly troubled with green water, suspect liver problems and visit your GP. If it is your pond that suffers from this green hue, then it is either the balance of plants, the soil used for their planting, or the location of your water feature that is incorrect. Never use ordinary garden soil or compost if you wish to introduce a new plant into your pond. The chances are this soil will contain too much nitrate or lime. Purchase a small bag of aquatic compost from the garden centre.

At a last resort you can buy algicides to deal with algae. Be very careful with the dosage of these chemicals. Too much will not only kill the algae but also half the neighbourhood. Complex pond filters and water sterilising units are also available but unnecessary in most small garden ponds.

A wildlife pond creates itself and will mature very quickly. Insects such as water boatmen, manic whirligig beetles and colourful damselflies will seem to appear from nowhere. Water snails, frogs and toads too seem to arrive unannounced. I recall discovering a small newt

"Your pond may need a good clean out once in a while"

swimming around in my wildlife pond only one month after its construction. He became something of a pet and I named him Tiny. After all, he was my newt.

Should you wish to introduce fish into your small pond, be careful not to overpopulate the water with them. There is, quite understandably, a finite amount of oxygen and food to go round. Too many fish can also cause the water to cloud. A couple of goldfish in any pond adds a sense of excitement as you see them dart through the water.

Any pool or garden pond can be improved by incorporating a small pump to create a flow of water. Small fountains, bought in association with the pump, can produce a cooling effect on a warm summer's day. Fountains, or even mini-cascades, push oxygen into the water and will benefit any plant and animal life. Submersible pumps usually come with a small filter attached to them. Try to raise the pump away from the floor of the pond by standing it on a brick. This will prevent any sediment becoming sucked into the filter when it is switched on. However, you will need to clean this filter a couple of times a year so make sure it is accessible. Do not try to emulate Jacques Cousteau's underwater efforts as you overstretch for the pump and tumble into your pond. Pumps can shift water a vertical height. Usually, the smaller the pump, the less is its capacity for doing work. Any reputable water garden centre will be able to give you advice on the size you will need. They will need to know what you intend using this pump for, its depth in the water and the vertical height you require this water to travel. Take along a sketch of your water design and any measurements. Some pumps have regulator valves on them that can control the flow of water. These are helpful if you have made a miscalculation and next door is complaining about their barbeque being extinguished each time your pump is switched on.

If you decide to include wood in your pond design, be aware that its surface becomes slippery when wet. This can be a safety issue, particularly when it is used in pond edging. A bridge or wooden stepping blocks can sometimes assist your passage into the water. Greater friction and anti-slip properties can be achieved by covering them with a mesh of galvanized chicken wire. Another point of caution is not to use treated railway sleepers as a pond border. They may leach toxic chemicals into the water over a period of time.

Simple water sculptures will need little maintenance during the course of a year. A quick clean and pump check will take about fifteen minutes. Ponds and pools will require little husbandry if you have followed advice about location, construction and planting. Ponds should be self-regulating but will require some assistance when leaf debris or the dreaded algae become a problem. In autumn and winter, a net can be spread across and above the water. Do not allow the net to accumulate too many leaves, otherwise it will have a teabag effect and foul water will seep out. Even if you have no trees in your garden, leaves will settle on this netting from surrounding areas.

You may be tempted to smash any ice that forms across your pond in winter. A hole in the ice will certainly

"Some water features don't please everyone"

benefit your submerged animal and plant life by allowing any unpleasant gases from the floor of the pond to escape. However, smashing the ice can damage the nervous system of any animal life and is not recommended. You would certainly take exception to your ice hole being struck with a hammer. So there! Ice only becomes a problem when it is over the water surface for a long period of time. If this is the case, then a kettle of boiling water will easily melt a tiny patch and set free these gases. Some people float a ball in their pond to provide a small patch of unfrozen water when the ball is removed.

Whatever water garden you choose - whether formal of informal, natural or architectural - it will provide you with enjoyment and pleasure. Stick to the fundamental advice about scale, position and planting, and you will discover it to be a valuable addition to your garden space.

The Ten Commandments for Water Gardens

1. When planning any water feature, remember its scale in your garden and its position.
2. If you have decided to construct a small pond, try to position it in the sunniest part of the garden.
3. Avoid building ponds or pools if you have small children in your family.
4. Try to visualise your pond or water feature in the garden before constructing it.
5. If cost is an issue, remember that either resin-bonded glass fibre and butyl will be more expensive than pre-cast plastic ponds. However, thin plastic ponds will be less durable.

6. Should you wish to include any electrical work in your design, always use the services of a qualified electrician.

7. Always provide a sand or liner quilt cushion for your pond, to avoid future puncture repairs.

8. When planting your pond, remember the value of oxygenators and surface plants to reduce algal bloom. Planting and patience!

9. Clean pumps and filters regularly to keep them efficient.

10. Any exposed water area in your aquatic feature will need netting in autumn and winter months to trap leaves and other debris.

8

Some Final Thoughts

If your partner has requested the sequel to '*Tess of the D'Urbervilles*' for her Christmas present and you purchase a book with the title: 'HARDY PERENNIALS FOREVER', alas, the ubiquitous insult 'gardening wally' could be justifiably levelled at you. However, do not be destroyed by the raft of humiliating belly laughs you receive on Christmas morning and jibes such as, 'It's time you subscribed to the Weeder's Digest,' or 'Have you ordered that tomato truss for your hernia yet?' Be bold and with a dignified reply tell them your days of gardening ignorance are over. You have now read this book and you positively overflow with gardening ideas and theory.

I would encourage everyone to at least have a try at gardening. You will certainly make mistakes in your first attempts. Everyone does. The salutary lesson means you will not make such errors again. Maybe your lettuce plants will not look as grand as those shown on the seed packet, but remember, that photograph was posed for by professional vegetables.

Some say gardening is a science. Indeed, there is knowledge required to practise some of its craft, but much of it is common sense. If you start to turn yellow, there is clearly something wrong with you. Suspect your gallbladder and await surgery. However, should your curly kale turn the colour of a banana, then a less drastic remedy of a liberal dose of Epsom salts is all that is required.

The negative attitude of 'Can't garden. Won't garden' is an easy way out and a defeatist ideology. This book will not arm you with the knowledge and potential to create the detail of an Italian Renaissance garden, nor will your application for the post of Head Gardener at RHS Wisley be successful. However, I hope its advice and suggestions will have boosted your confidence and encourage you to get out there and try new things.

Gardening should be an exercise designed not to put you in the high dependency unit of your local hospital. If it does, you clearly have too big a garden or you are a crisis gardener. Coping with your garden means being organized and understanding there are areas of your garden unable to look after themselves. If you keep chickens, they require minimal attention on a regular basis. The same pragmatic approach applies to plants.

You may suffer from hay fever and refuse to venture into the garden. The high pollen counts would seem to indicate plants are having more sex than you. The days of having a runny nose and congested eyes are few in number, so remember, you can try to reverse the situation in the autumn and winter months.

I attended an 'open gardens' day in the village where I live. One of the show garden participants was a lady with all the charm and appeal of Pol Pot. She spoke with such a volume you could hear her in Antarctica, and her demeanour reflected the sensitivity of a Great White shark. I overheard her bullying a rather timid visitor, keen to learn the secret of her horticultural success.

'I utterly forbid you to be half-hearted about gardening,' she proclaimed.

'You see, you've got to love your garden, young man, whether you like it or not!'

To quote Kurt Vonnegut, 'So it goes.'

Happy gardening!

Lightning Source UK Ltd.
Milton Keynes UK
UKOW03f2111250314

228784UK00001B/2/P